THE CREATION OF A EUROPEAN LAW OF CONTRACTS - THE ROLE OF STANDARD FORM CONTRACTS AND PRINCIPLES OF INTERPRETATION

SERIE ONDERNEMING EN RECHT

onder redactie van

Prof. S.C.J.J. Kortmann
N.E.D. Faber

deel 28

THE CREATION OF A EUROPEAN LAW OF CONTRACTS - THE ROLE OF STANDARD FORM CONTRACTS AND PRINCIPLES OF INTERPRETATION

by

Ewan McKendrick

Holder of the CPO *wisselleerstoel* during the academic years 2002-2003 and 2003-2004, Faculty of Law, University of Nijmegen, The Netherlands

Professor of English Private Law, University of Oxford and Fellow of Lady Margaret Hall

KLUWER - DEVENTER - 2004

ISBN 90 130 19145

Willy Cremers, grafisch ontwerp
Gonnie Jakobs, lay-out tekst

PREFACE BY THE SERIES' EDITORS

Standard terms are an important part of commercial contracts. This is certainly true for cross-border transactions. The practical significance of boilerplate clauses may even outweigh that of the default rules of the laws governing these contracts.

Standard terms are the central theme of the inaugural lecture given by Professor Ewan McKendrick, Professor of English Private Law at the University of Oxford, as the new holder of the Nijmegen 'CPO *wissel-leerstoel*' (chair established by the Centre for Post-graduate legal Education) of the Nijmegen University. This book is an elaborated version of the inaugural lecture. In a captivating triptych the author discusses (i) the significance of the standard terms in modern commercial contracts, (ii) the importance of the rules or principles applied by the courts when interpreting contractual documents, and (iii) the significance of the regulation of standard terms within national legal systems, particularly by way of mandatory rules.

McKendrick convincingly demonstrates that greater importance should be given to standard terms (or boilerplate clauses) when teaching the law of contract. Furthermore, he suggests that the rules and principles applied by the courts when interpreting contracts assume considerable significance in view of the harmonisation of contract law in Europe. Finally, he demonstrates the significance of mandatory rules, in particular those rules which regulate the fairness of standard contract terms, and suggests that steps ought to be taken, as far as possible, to harmonise these mandatory rules within Europe.

The observations of Professor Ewan McKendrick are of great interest to academic lawyers and practitioners throughout Europe. With great pleasure we include this book in our series.

Nijmegen, The Netherlands,
November 2004

Professor Sebastian Kortmann
Chairman of the Board of the
Business and Law Research Centre

Dennis Faber
Director of the Business
and Law Research Centre

CONTENTS

THE CREATION OF A EUROPEAN LAW OF CONTRACTS - THE ROLE OF STANDARD FORM CONTRACTS AND PRINCIPLES OF INTERPRETATION

Introduction		1
I	The importance of standard terms	5
	a An incomplete picture of the law	6
	b An understanding of transactions	16
II	Interpretation	27
	a The meaning of documents and the intention of the parties	32
	b Commercial construction and re-writing the contract	37
	c Pre-contractual negotiations	40
	d A common meaning for common terms	43
III	Regulation and mandatory rules	47
Conclusion		53

THE CREATION OF A EUROPEAN LAW OF CONTRACTS - THE ROLE OF STANDARD FORM CONTRACTS AND PRINCIPLES OF INTERPRETATION

THE CREATION OF A EUROPEAN LAW OF CONTRACTS - THE ROLE OF STANDARD FORM CONTRACTS AND PRINCIPLES OF INTERPRETATION

INTRODUCTION

The relationship between legal education and legal practice has not always been an easy one. The gulf between the two worlds has sometimes been wide and there is a need for a bridge to span the divide because the reality is that legal education and legal practice have a great deal to learn from one another. While the role of the jurist and the practitioner are distinct, they are nevertheless complementary and should be co-operative and not competitive[1]. In this respect it is a particular pleasure for me to be able to accept the appointment to the CPO Chair in this distinguished University. This appointment enables me to teach, and to learn from, both students and practitioners. I have been appointed to teach the law of contract, in particular the English law of contract, and I shall adopt the same approach to my teaching, whether teaching law students or legal practitioners. It is my belief that the law of contract is best taught in a transactional context. For law students, this means that they must learn to see the rules of the law of contract in their transactional context; too often students are taught legal doctrine in a vacuum, divorced from the context in which the rules operate. Practitioners, on the other hand, need to be reminded of the significance of legal rules and the way in which they impact on legal practice. A secure grasp of legal principle is an important part of the armoury of the legal practitioner. Analysing the operation of legal rules in a transactional context can therefore be a fruitful learning experience both for the legal practitioner and the law student.

---

1   I have borrowed the terminology from Lord Goff in his essay 'The Search for Principle' which is re-printed in W. Swadling and G. Jones (eds.) *The Search for Principle: Essays in Honour of Lord Goff of Chieveley* (Oxford, 1999) 313, 329 where, speaking of the respective roles of the judge and the jurist, he states that their roles 'though distinct, are complementary: they should be co-operative, not competitive.'

The focus of this lecture is on the standard terms to be found in modern commercial contracts. These standard terms are commonly referred to as 'boilerplate clauses'. While these terms are of enormous significance in commercial practice, they do not always receive the attention which they deserve in scholarly writing on the law of contract. Textbooks, monographs and practitioner works (at least in England) tend to focus on the black-letter rules that make up the law of contract and not upon the terms that are commonly to be found in modern commercial contracts. The same tendency can be seen in much of the current debate on the harmonisation of private law within Europe and beyond. When we focus on harmonisation we tend to concentrate on the black-letter rules, whether these rules are legally binding, as in most national legal systems, or non-binding, as in the case of the Principles of European Contract Law or the UNIDROIT Principles of International Commercial Contracts. The debate on harmonisation has not given standard contract terms the attention that they deserve. Indeed, a plausible argument can be made to the effect that harmonisation is more likely to take place as a result of the increasing use of standard terms in commercial contracts. Most major law firms and commercial parties have their own standard terms of business which they seek to use in the transactions which they conclude. Although there are undoubtedly differences between these standard terms, their similarities tend to be greater than their differences. These boilerplate clauses are as important, if not more important, than the black-letter rules found in national legal systems. In this respect, we have to remember that most contract rules in national laws are default rules; that is to say, they apply unless they are excluded by the terms of the contract. Mandatory rules, at least in the commercial context, are relatively few. This being the case, the rules of law can be, and frequently are, displaced by the terms of the contract concluded between the parties. Thus it is the terms of the contract, rather than the rules of law, that play the principal role in the regulation of the relationship between the parties[2].

This lecture is divided into three parts. The first part seeks to demonstrate the significance of the standard terms to be found in modern

---

2   Of course, the point can be made that, in practice, contracting parties frequently rely
     on informal understandings and not upon the written terms of the deal. While this
     is undoubtedly true, it is not my intention in this lecture to deal with such informal
     understandings, on which see generally D Campbell, H Collins and J Wightman
     (eds.) *Implicit Dimensions of Contract* (Oxford, Hart, 2003).

commercial contracts and their importance for legal education. The argument will be that we should make greater use of standard terms (or boilerplate clauses) when teaching the law of contract. The second and the third part seek to explore two of the legal issues that arise from the claim that greater attention ought to be given to these standard terms. The first legal issue, explored in part two, is the importance of the rules or principles applied by the courts when interpreting contractual documents. Given the widespread use of boilerplate clauses, and the fact that issues of interpretation or construction are commonly raised in modern litigation, the rules applied by the courts when interpreting contract terms can be seen to assume considerable significance. If the same clause is interpreted in different ways by courts in different jurisdictions then greater difficulties are created for commercial parties and their lawyers. On the other hand, if the clause is interpreted in the same way in different jurisdictions, then it becomes possible to develop a set of standard terms that can be used in a broader range of international or transnational transactions. The third part deals, albeit more briefly, with the significance of the regulation of standard terms within national legal systems, particularly by way of mandatory rules. Mandatory rules can create difficulties for commercial parties because they can and do result in the invalidation of some of the terms to be found in commercial contracts. If the mandatory rules are the same within different nation states then the practical problems are likely to be reduced and contracting parties can draft their standard terms in the light of these mandatory rules. On the other hand, if the mandatory rules vary from State to State, the difficulties caused are much greater because commercial parties must then find out which mandatory rules operate within which legal system and adapt their standard terms on a jurisdiction by jurisdiction basis in order to comply with them.

I   THE IMPORTANCE OF STANDARD TERMS

The first part of the lecture is devoted to the importance of the standard terms to be found in modern commercial contracts. However, it is not my intention to seek to prove their importance empirically. To my knowledge, no such study has ever been carried out. But we know that most, if not all, major law firms have their standard-form (or boilerplate) clauses and many major commercial parties also have their own standard terms of business. Such standard terms assume different forms. Some are produced by the particular commercial party and are used, or sought to be used, in all contracts concluded by that party. The widespread use of these terms has given rise to what lawyers call the 'battle of the forms'[3] as parties battle it out in an attempt to ensure that their terms govern any deal that is made between them. Other standard terms are industry-wide in the sense that they are used by most participants in the industry and are not peculiar to the particular contracting party. Some of these industry-wide clauses have been approved by regulators, others have not. The precise content of these standard terms differs from industry to industry but there is nevertheless a high degree of similarity between them, at least in the sense that they tend to deal with the same issues.

An illustration of this is provided by Schmitthoff's *Export Trade: The Law and Practice of International Trade*[4] which includes the following clauses in a list which should be incorporated by an exporter into its general terms of business: a general clause (which subjects every contract of sale to the seller's conditions of sale), a retention of title clause, a price escalation clause, a clause making provision for the payment of interest in the event of the buyer failing to make punctual payment of the price, a force majeure clause, a choice of law clause, an arbitration clause and a jurisdiction clause. Other clauses could be added to this list, such as an exclusion or limitation clause, a hardship clause, an entire agreement clause, an assignment clause (or a clause which prohibits assignment) and a liquidated damages clause.

---

3   See, for example, *Butler Machine Tool Co Ltd v. Ex-Cell-O Corporation* [1979] 1 WLR 401; Principles of European Contract Law, Articles 2:208 and 2:209 and UNIDROIT Principles for International Commercial Contracts Article 2.11.

4   (10th edn, 2000) paras 32-014 and 32-015.

While these clauses are prevalent in practice, they do not feature so widely in textbooks on the law of contract or in legal education. While there are notable exceptions[5] most textbooks focus on the black-letter rules of contract law and the same can be said of most undergraduate courses on the law of contract, at least in universities in England and Wales. Undergraduate students enrolled on a traditional undergraduate course on the law of contract rarely encounter standard contract terms[6]. They are more likely to encounter such terms in the context of more specialised courses. Thus choice of law clauses and jurisdiction clauses will be found in courses on private international law or, to use the title more commonly used in England, the conflict of laws. Retention of title clauses feature in courses on insolvency law and the law of trusts[7]. Arbitration is now a specialist option, largely, if not exclusively, found on post-graduate courses. It may be said that the omission of standard form clauses from undergraduate legal education does not really matter. I wish to suggest that it does matter and that it matters for two reasons. The first is that a failure to examine standard contract terms will give to students an incomplete picture of the law and the second is that an understanding of contract terms is an integral part of any examination of the structure and content of modern transactions. I shall now examine these reasons in more detail.

(a)   An incomplete picture of the law

The claim that a failure to have regard to the significance of standard contract terms gives an incomplete picture of the law of contract, in the sense that it gives us at best a partial grasp of the issues that arise in the case-law, can be illustrated by reference to the case of *J Lauritzen AS v. Wijsmuller BV (The 'Super Servant Two')*[8]. The defendants, Wijsmuller,

---

5   See, for example, R Christou *Boilerplate: Practical Clauses* London, (Sweet & Maxwell, 3rd edn, 2002).

6   An exception is, perhaps, the general clause mentioned in Schmitthoff. While the general clause tends not to be examined as such, it may appear in undergraduate courses in the context of a battle of the forms case. But even there the focus will tend to be upon the rules of offer and acceptance and not upon the purpose that is sought to be achieved by the general clause.

7   While trusts is a compulsory subject in England and Wales, not all courses on the law of trusts examine retention of title in any detail.

8   [1990] 1 Lloyd's Rep 1.

agreed to carry the plaintiffs' drilling rig from Japan to Rotterdam. The contract, dated 7 July 1980, provided that the rig would be delivered between 20 June and 20 August 1981 and that it would be carried using either Super Servant One or Super Servant Two in Wijsmuller's option. Both of these vessels were large, self-propelled, semi-submersible barges built for carrying large loads such as the drilling rig in the present case. Clause 17 of the contract, which is set out below, gave the defendants the right to cancel the contract in the event of *force majeure* or any other circumstance which reasonably prevented the performance of the contract. The defendants claimed that by November 1980 they had made an internal decision, which they admitted was not irrevocable, to schedule Super Servant Two to transport the plaintiffs' rig and to allocate Super Servant One to the performance of other concluded contracts. On 29 January 1981 Super Servant Two sank and became a total loss while transporting another rig in the Zaire River. On 16 February 1981 the defendants told the plaintiffs that they could not carry the plaintiffs' rig using either Super Servant One or Super Servant Two. They could not use Super Servant One because it was required for the performance of other contracts which the defendants had concluded and they could not use Super Servant Two because it was a total loss. The parties then entered into 'without prejudice negotiations' after which rig was towed by the defendants, using a more expensive method of transportation.

The plaintiffs alleged that the defendants' failure to transport the rig in the agreed manner was a breach of contract so that the defendants were liable for the additional costs that had been incurred in transporting the rig. The defendants denied liability to pay damages on two grounds. The first was that they alleged that the contract between the parties had been frustrated, that is to say it had been discharged as a matter of law on the ground that performance of the contract according to its terms had become impossible[9]. This is the defence which is discussed in most text-

---

9   The doctrine of frustration is not confined to cases of impossibility but operates within very narrow limits. It operates to discharge a contract where, after the formation of the contract, something occurs which renders performance of the contract impossible, illegal, or something radically different from that which was in the contemplation of the parties at the time of entry into the contract: see further E McKendrick *Contract Law: Text, Cases and Materials* (Oxford, 2003), chapter 23.

book accounts of the case[10]. For our purposes, the more significant defence is that based on clause 17 of the contract. It is necessary to set out clause 17.1 in full. It stated:

17. *Cancellation*

17.1. Wijsmuller has the right to cancel its performance under this Contract whether the loading has been completed or not, in the event of force majeur (sic), Acts of God, perils or danger and accidents of the sea, acts of war, warlike-operations, acts of public enemies, restraint of princes, rulers or people or seizure under legal process, quarantine restrictions, civil commotions, blockade, strikes, lockout, closure of the Suez or Panama Canal, congestion of harbours or any other circumstances whatsoever, causing extra-ordinary periods of delay and similar events and/or circumstances, abnormal increases in prices and wages, scarcity of fuel and similar events, which reasonably may impede, prevent or delay the performance of this contract.

The Court of Appeal held, affirming the decision of Hobhouse J at first instance[11], that the defendants were entitled to rely on clause 17 of the contract in order to absolve themselves from liability to pay damages to the plaintiffs provided that the sinking of Super Servant Two occurred without negligence on the part of the defendants, their employees or agents but that they were not entitled to invoke the doctrine of frustration in order to justify their failure to tow the rig in the agreed manner.

Although the doctrine of frustration is not presently our prime concern, it is necessary to give brief consideration to the reasons given for the inability of the defendants to rely on the doctrine of frustration because it helps to explain why it is that force majeure clauses play such an important role in commercial practice in England. Two reasons were given by the judges. The first was that, in so far as the sinking of the Super Servant Two was attributable to the negligence of the defendants or their

---

10   See, for example, G Treitel *The Law of Contract* (London, Sweet & Maxwell, 11th edn, 2003) pp. 907-908 (although clause 17 is discussed at other points in the book, see pp. 224 and 778); J Beatson *Anson's Law of Contract* (Oxford, 28th edn, 2002) pp. 551-552; J C Smith: *Smith and Thomas: A Casebook on Contract* (London, Sweet & Maxwell, 11th edn, 2000) pp. 547-551 and Cheshire, Fifoot and Furmston's *Law of Contract* (London, Butterworths, 14th edn, 2001) p.642). A partial exception is H G Beale, W D Bishop and M P Furmston *Contract: Cases and Materials* (London, Butterworths, 4th edn, 2001) pp. 469-472. Rather curiously, the authors set out clause 17 of the contract but omit the sections of the judgment which deal with the interpretation of the clause.
11   [1989] 1 Lloyd's Rep 148.

employees, such negligence operated to exclude the operation of the doctrine of frustration[12]. The doctrine of frustration is concerned with events that are beyond the control of the parties; it does not extend to events that are within their control, albeit that they fail to exercise that control with reasonable care and skill[13]. The second reason was that the cause of the non-performance of the contract was held to be the 'decision' of the defendants not to employ Super Servant One in the performance of the contract with the plaintiffs and not the sinking of the Super Servant Two. This was held to be sufficient to prevent the operation of the doctrine of frustration because it was held that the essence of the doctrine of frustration 'should not be due to the act or election of the party seeking to rely on it'[14] and it must be some 'outside event or extraneous change of situation'[15]. This emphasis on the 'decision' or the 'choice' of the defendants may seem at first sight to be surprising because the defendants did not appear to have a choice in any meaningful sense of that word. They were left with one functioning barge and that barge could not perform the work of two. In so far as they could be said to have had a choice, it was a choice as to which contract not to perform. But, according to the Court of Appeal in the present case, the law does not require the existence of a meaningful choice; the mere existence of a choice was sufficient to shut out the operation of the doctrine of frustration[16].

Thus *Super Servant Two* provides us with an illustration of the narrow limits within which the doctrine of frustration operates in English contract law. As Bingham LJ observed, the doctrine of frustration is 'not to be lightly invoked, must be kept within very narrow limits and ought

---

12   [1990] 1 Lloyd's Rep 1, 10.

13   *Joseph Constantine Steamship Ltd v Imperial Smelting Corp Ltd* [1942] AC 154.

14   *Hirji Mulji v Cheong Yue Steamship Co Ltd* [1926] AC 497, 510; *Davis Contractors Ltd v Fareham UDC* [1956] AC 696, 729.

15   *The Hannah Blumenthal* [1983] 1 AC 854, 909.

16   Cases which were relied upon to support the proposition that the defendants could invoke the doctrine of frustration provided that they had acted reasonably in their allocation of Super Servant One were distinguished on the ground that they were concerned with the interpretation of force majeure clauses and not with the doctrine of frustration: see, for example, *Bremer Handelsgesellschaft mbH v Continental Grain Co* [1983] 1 Lloyd's Rep 269; *Intertradex SA v Lesier-Toureaux SARL* [1978] 2 Lloyd's Rep 509.

not to be extended'[17]. There are a number of reasons for this restrictive approach. The first is the need to promote certainty in commercial transactions. The courts do not wish to provide an easy escape route for a party which discovers that it has entered into a bad bargain. Accordingly, the threshold set by the doctrine of frustration is a high one. Secondly, liability for breach of contract is generally strict in English law and is not dependent upon proof that the party alleged to be in breach was at fault. This being the case, it is not generally a defence for a defendant to state that it acted reasonably or prudently in the circumstances in which it found itself. Liability is based on its failure to provide the promised level of performance and the reasons for that non-performance are, generally speaking, irrelevant. The third is that the consequences of the operation of the doctrine are drastic in the sense that frustration operates to bring the contract between the parties to an end automatically, irrespective of their wishes[18]. Given that the sanction is such a drastic one, the courts are, perhaps understandably, reluctant to invoke it.

In what sense can it be said that *Super Servant Two* illustrates the proposition that a failure to have regard to the standard terms of a contract gives us an 'incomplete picture' of the law? The answer to this question lies in the fact that, as we have noted, textbook discussion of the case has focused principally on the legal doctrine of frustration, whereas the real key to the case lies, not in the doctrine of frustration, but in clause 17. It was clause 17 that offered the defendants some hope of salvation and the court concluded that the defendants were entitled to invoke clause 17 in order to deny liability in damages provided that the sinking of Super Servant Two was not attributable to the negligence of the defendants, their employees or agents. Three points are worth noting in relation to clause 17.

The first is that the court reached the conclusion that clause 17 did not extend to the negligence of the defendants as a matter of construction, or interpretation of the clause, and did not derive its conclusion as a matter of law from the use of the words 'force majeure'[19]. The reason for

---

17   [1990] 1 Lloyd's Rep 1, 8, citing *Bank Line Ltd v. Arthur Capel & Co* [1919] AC 435, 459; *Davis Contractors Ltd v Fareham UDC* [1956] AC 696, 715 and *Pioneer Shipping Ltd v B T P Tioxide Ltd (The Nema)* [1982] AC 724, 752.

18   *Hirji Mulji v Cheong Yue Steamship Co Ltd* [1926] AC 497, 505, 509.

19   Although the words 'force majeure' were in fact spelt incorrectly in the clause, where they appeared as 'force majeur'.

this is that English law does not recognise the existence of a legal doctrine known as force majeure[20]. The words 'force majeure' have no fixed meaning as a matter of law[21]. Rather, their meaning must be ascertained in the light of the context in which the words are in fact used[22]. Generally, that context will indicate that what the parties had in mind was events that were beyond the (reasonable) control of the parties. This point can be demonstrated by reference to the facts of the present case. The Court of Appeal concluded that the words 'perils or danger and accidents of the sea' in clause 17 did not, as a matter of interpretation, include the sinking of Super Servant Two when the cause of the sinking was the negligence of the defendants, their employees or agents[23]. While the words 'perils or danger and accidents of the sea' could, read alone, encompass events that are attributable to the fault of one of the contracting parties, Bingham LJ concluded that 'the words are not to be read alone but as part of a contract to be construed as a whole'[24]. An important factor which persuaded the court to conclude that the parties did not intend these words to extend to negligence was that almost all of the events listed in clause 17 were events which were beyond the direct or indirect control of the defendants[25]. This being the case, the inference to be drawn was that the clause as a whole was confined to such events and did not extend to events occasioned by the negligence of the defendants. Given that most force majeure clauses focus upon events which are beyond the control of the parties, the effect of this approach is generally to take negligently inflicted damage outside the ambit of a force majeure clause unless the word 'negligence' or a synonym for negligence is expressly incorporated into the clause. But it is important to note that this conclusion was reached as a matter of construction, not law, so that it would have been possible to draft clause 17

---

20 *Matsoukis v Priestman* [1915] 1 KB 681, 685.

21 *Thomas Borthwick (Glasgow) Ltd v Faure Fairclough Ltd* [1968] 1 Lloyd's Rep 16, 28.

22 *Lebeaupin v Richard Crispin & Co* [1920] 2 KB 714, 720.

23 This is consistent with the general reluctance of the courts to reach the conclusion that one party has agreed to exempt the other from liability for the consequences of his negligence unless clear words are used to that effect in the contract: see, for example, *Canada Steamship Lines Ltd v The King* [1952] AC 192.

24 [1990] 1 Lloyd's Rep 1, 6.

25 Thus Bingham LJ observed (at p. 7) that 'the general tenor of the clause, opening with a reference to force majeure and acts of God and including such events as acts of war, civil commotion, canal closure and harbour congestion, strongly points towards events beyond the direct or indirect control of Wijsmuller'.

in such a way as to include negligence within its scope (for example, by re-phrasing the clause so that it read 'perils or dangers and accidents of the sea (whether caused by negligence or not)'). The inclusion of the words in brackets might well be resisted by the other party to the contract in the negotiation process, but that is a matter which concerns the bargaining strength of the parties. There is no rule of law which states that it is impossible to include an event which is within one party's control within the scope of a force majeure clause.

Secondly, the case illustrates the relative insignificance of the words 'force majeure' in clause 17. The battleground, in terms of litigation, tends to be the events listed in the clause and not the words 'force majeure' themselves. Thus on the facts of *Super Servant Two* the dispute between the parties centred on the meaning of the words 'perils or danger and accidents of the sea'. No significance at all was attached by the judges to the words 'force majeure' except, perhaps, to indicate in general terms the type of event that fell within the scope of the clause. This is a potential source of confusion in relation to transactions concluded between continental lawyers and common lawyers. The continental lawyer may conclude that the words 'force majeure' by definition are confined to events that are beyond the control of the parties[26], whereas an English lawyer will have no such pre-disposition and is more likely to conclude that the scope of the clause will be defined by the list of events contained within the clause.

Thirdly, clause 17 demonstrates that parties can and do insert force majeure or hardship clauses[27] into their contracts and that their ability to do so is an important factor in terms of explaining the narrow scope within which the doctrine of frustration presently operates. As has been noted, the courts do not wish to allow the doctrine of frustration to be invoked by a party who is looking for a way out of bargain that has turned

---

[26]   This may not necessarily be so because the content of a particular force majeure clause may in fact be broader than the concept of force majeure that is recognised in a national law.

[27]   A hardship clause is a clause in a contract which states that, in the event of significant hardship which makes it more onerous for one party to perform its obligations under the contract (or some similar event), the parties agree to enter into negotiations with a view to adjusting the contract in order to reduce or alleviate the hardship (or they agree that a third party shall have the power to resolve the matter). Thus it is a clause which typically makes provision for the renegotiation of the contract rather than its termination or suspension.

out to be a bad one. But the same objection obviously does not apply to a clause which has been agreed by the parties to the contract and which exempts the parties from liability for non-performance in certain defined circumstances. In such a case the court is not involved in making a new contract for the parties but is carrying out the traditional function of the court in terms of ascertaining and giving effect to the agreement that the parties have in fact reached. This being the case, a party which wishes to provide itself with some protection in the event of it being unable to perform its obligations under the contract would be well-advised to insert an appropriately drafted force majeure or hardship clause into the contract. This point was recognised by Hobhouse J at first instance in *Super Servant Two* when he stated that if a party wishes to obtain protection in the event of a partial failure of its supplies, it 'must bargain for the inclusion of a suitable force majeure clause in the contract'[28].

Force majeure clauses therefore play an important role in modern commercial contracts governed by English law. A number of reasons can be advanced for this development. First, a force majeure clause provides the parties with greater certainty. The scope of the doctrine of frustration is to some extent uncertain. For example, there was substantial litigation over the question of whether or not the closure of the Suez Canal in 1956 operated to frustrate contracts for the carriage of goods by a route which would normally include use of the Suez Canal[29]. The House of Lords concluded that the increased cost of carrying the goods round the Cape of Good Hope did not operate to frustrate the contract because there was not a sufficiently fundamental change in the nature of the obligation assumed. Rather than engage in litigation over whether or not the contract has been frustrated, the parties can include, as was the case with clause 17 of the contract in *Super Servant Two*, the closure of the Suez Canal in the list of events which are to count as force majeure events. In this way uncertainty can be reduced by the incorporation of a suitably drafted force majeure clause in the contract. The clause can specify the circumstances in which it is to operate and the role of the court is then reduced to the interpretation of the clause. This leads us on the second advantage of a force

---

28   [1989] 1 Lloyd's Rep 148, 158.
29   *Tsakiroglou & Co Ltd v Noblee & Thorl GmbH* [1962] AC 93; *Ocean Tramp Tankers Corporation v v/o Sovfracht (The Eugenia)* [1964] 2 QB 226. Litigation on this issue also took place in the United States of America: see, for example, *Transatlantic Financing v US* 363 F 2d 312 (1966).

majeure clause which is that it gives contracting parties the opportunity, should they wish to avail themselves of it, to escape from the narrowness of the doctrine of frustration by including within their force majeure clause an event, such as the closure of the Suez Canal, which would not, at common law, be sufficient to frustrate the contract. Thirdly, a force majeure clause offers to the parties greater remedial flexibility. One of the problems with the doctrine of frustration is that it is extremely inflexible in that it brings the contract to an end, irrespective of the wishes of the parties to the contract[30]. Force majeure clauses, on the other hand, offer to the parties a high degree of remedial flexibility in that they can decide for themselves the consequences which are to flow from the occurrence of a force majeure event. For example, a force majeure clause can provide that, on the occurrence of a force majeure event, there is to be an extension of time for performance, the suspension or variation of the contract or even the termination or cancellation of the contract.

Thus it is that force majeure clauses and hardship clauses are a regular feature of commercial contracts governed by English law. And, the greater the provision made in the contract for the occurrence of events which may make performance of the contract more onerous for one or both of the contracting parties, the less likely it is that the contract will be frustrated. The reason for this is that a contract will not be frustrated where express provision has been made in the contract for the alleged frustrating event[31]. Take the example of the closure of the Suez Canal. Would such a closure have operated to frustrate the contract between the parties in *Super Servant Two*? The answer is that it would not because the contract itself, in clause 17, made provision for the consequences of the closure of the Suez Canal. Closure gave to the defendants the right to cancel the contract. This being the case, the contract between the parties would not have been frustrated. In other words, the task of the lawyer is first to have regard to the terms of the contract that have been agreed between the parties. In many cases the contract itself will tell the lawyer what is to happen on the occurrence of events such as strikes, Acts of God etc. The lawyer then simply has to give effect to the agreement of the parties. In these circumstances there is simply no room for the doctrine of frustration to operate because the contract provides the answer. However

---

30   *Hirji Mulji v Cheong Yue Steamship Co Ltd* [1926] AC 497, 505, 509.
31   *Metropolitan Water Board v Dick Kerr and Co* [1918] AC 119.

a force majeure clause will not operate to exclude the doctrine of frustration in all cases. In some cases, doubtless rare, the event will be of such magnitude as to take it outside the scope of the force majeure clause. The fact that most force majeure clauses make provision for the suspension of the contract on the occurrence of a force majeure event indicates that the parties probably have in mind events, such as a strike, which can be resolved within the time-frame laid down in the clause. But where the event renders further performance of the contract unthinkable, the court may conclude that the contract has in fact been frustrated. Thus a force majeure clause which includes in the list of force majeure events 'strikes' and 'wars' may be held, as a matter of interpretation, not to cover a protracted national strike, such as a general strike, or a war of the magnitude of the first or second world war[32]. Such catastrophic events are, however, comparatively rare. Most of the events that occur will fall within the scope of an appropriately drafted force majeure or hardship clause. As contracts make provision for the occurrence of a greater range of events, so the scope for the application of the doctrine of frustration diminishes. In most cases the inquiry will start and finish with the terms of the contract itself.

The significance of force majeure clauses ought to be reflected in textbooks on the law of contract and in our teaching of the subject. But this has not happened. Very often they are not mentioned at all. The leading textbooks do contain references to force majeure clauses, but they are usually brief. The following is an example:

> 'In this chapter we trace the history of the doctrine [of frustration] and examine the scope of its present application. It should, however, be noted that as the doctrine has developed, so too has the use, particularly in standard form contracts of force majeure clauses, which entitle one or both of the parties to be excused (in whole or in part) from performance of the contract. Such clauses may cover non-frustrating events and may provide for more flexible remedies than total discharge. For instance they may entitle a party to suspend performance, to claim an extension of time for performance, or to be compensated for performance which will be more onerous.'[33]

Immediately following the latter sentence is a footnote which states, 'such clauses fall outside the scope of the book.' While this brief mention of the

---

32   See, for example, *Fibrosa Spolka Akcyjna v. Fairbairn Lawson Combe Barbour Ltd* [1943] A.C. 32, 40-41.
33   J Beatson *Anson's Law of Contract* (28th edn, 2002) p. 531.

15

role of force majeure clauses is an important step in the right direction, more ought to be done because, in the absence of a substantial discussion of the role of force majeure clauses, students are given an incomplete picture of the law and its operation in practice.

(b)   An understanding of transactions

Secondly, a focus on standard contract terms is an important element when seeking to understand the structure and content of modern commercial transactions. Too often students are encouraged to focus on the rule of law for which a case stands as authority and do not take sufficient account of the terms of the contract itself. Yet contract cases are not decided in a vacuum; they are decided in a transactional context and it is important to examine that context, in particular the structure and content of the terms that are the subject of the litigation. A case which illustrates the importance of a careful examination of the terms of the contract is *L Schuler AG v. Wickman Machine Tool Sales Ltd*[34]. On 1 May 1963 the parties entered into a 'distributorship agreement' under which Schuler granted to Wickman (referred to in the contract as 'Sales') the sole right to sell Schuler products, including panel presses, in a specified territory, which included the United Kingdom. The critical terms of the contract, the meaning of which were in dispute between the parties, were clauses 7(b) and 11.

-   Clause 7(b) provided:

    (b) It shall be condition of this Agreement that:

    (i) Sales shall send its representatives to visit the six firms whose names are listed in the Schedule hereto at least once in every week for the purpose of soliciting orders for panel presses;

    (ii) that the same representative shall visit each firm on each occasion unless there are unavoidable reasons preventing the visit being made by that representative in which case the visit shall be made by an alternate representative and Sales will ensure that such a visit is always made by the same alternate representative.

-   Clause 11, which dealt with the duration of the agreement, provided:

---

34   [1974] AC 235.

(a) This Agreement and the rights granted hereunder to Sales shall commence on the First day of May 1963 and shall continue in force (unless previously determined as hereinafter provided) until the 31st day of December 1967 and thereafter unless and until determined by either party upon giving to the other not less than 12 months' notice in writing to that effect expiring on the said 31st day of December 1967 or any subsequent anniversary thereof PROVIDED that Schuler or Sales may by notice in writing to the other determine this Agreement forthwith if:

(i) the other shall have committed a material breach of its obligations hereunder and shall have failed to remedy the same within 60 days of being required in writing so to do or

(ii) the other shall cease to carry on business or shall enter into liquidation (other than a members' voluntary liquidation for the purposes of reconstruction or amalgamation) or shall suffer the appointment of a Receiver of the whole or a material part of its undertaking;

and PROVIDED FURTHER that Schuler may by notice determine this Agreement forthwith if Sales shall cease to be a wholly-owned subsidiary of Wickman Limited.

(b) The termination of this Agreement shall be without prejudice to any rights or liabilities accrued due prior to the date of termination and the terms contained herein as to discount commission or otherwise will apply to any orders placed by Sales with Schuler and accepted by Schuler before such termination.

The six firms mentioned in clause 7(b) were six of the largest motor manufacturers in the United Kingdom. Initially, Wickman failed to make a number of the visits required by clause 7: its failures were described by Lord Reid as 'fairly extensive'[35]. The parties entered into negotiations with a view to improving the position and thereafter it did improve but 'there were still a considerable number of failures'[36] on the part of Wickman. On 27 October 1964 Schuler wrote a letter to Wickman in which it purported to terminate the agreement between the parties on the ground that Wickman had failed to fulfil its obligation to make the specified weekly visits. The contract between the parties contained an arbitration clause and Wickman commenced proceedings against Schuler in which it alleged that

---

35   [1974] AC 235.

36   *Ibid.* A rather more benevolent approach was taken by Lord Denning in the Court of Appeal: see Wickman Machine Tool Sales Ltd v. L Schuler A G [1972] 1 WLR 840, 848 where he records that in the period from 14 July to 27 October Wickman 'did well' with their visiting, that only 9 visits were missed during this period and that there were 'good reasons' for the missed visits.

Schuler had wrongfully purported to terminate the contract between the parties and had thereby repudiated the contract. Schuler admitted that it had terminated the agreement but submitted that it was entitled to do so under clause 11(a)(i) and clause 7(b)[37]. The arbitrator held that Schuler was not entitled to terminate the agreement under either clause. In relation to the clause 7(b) issue he declined to hold that any breach of the clause entitled Schuler to terminate the contract. In relation to clause 11(a)(i) he distinguished between two periods of time. He held that Wickman's failure to visit the six firms in the period between 1 May 1963 and 13 January 1964 constituted a material breach of the contract but held that these breaches had been waived by Schuler. However, in relation to the period between 13 January and 27 October 1964 he found that the performance of Wickman had improved considerably and, while there were a small number of missed visits, these failures did not constitute a material breach within the terms of clause 11. Schuler challenged the award and in the High Court Mr Justice Mocatta held that Schuler was in fact entitled to terminate the agreement as a result of Wickman's breach of clause 7(b)[38]. Wickman then appealed to the Court of Appeal where the finding of Mr Justice Mocatta was reversed and the award of the arbitrator restored[39]. Schuler appealed to the House of Lords and submitted that it was entitled to terminate the contract pursuant to clause 7(b)[40]. The appeal was, however, dismissed so that Schuler was held not to be entitled to terminate further performance of the contract as a result of Wickman's breach of clause 7(b).

It can be seen that a central issue at each stage in the proceedings was whether or not Schuler was entitled to terminate further performance

---

[37]   Initially, Schuler pleaded that it was entitled to terminate the agreement pursuant to clause 11(a)(i). No reliance was placed in the defence on clause 7(b) until 'some days' into the arbitration (see [1972] 1 WLR 840, 849) when it amended its defence so as to rely on clause 7(b). The fact that clause 7(b) was not invoked until such a late stage in the proceedings probably did not help Schuler when making its submissions to the court. That said, the conduct of the parties subsequent to the making of the contract is inadmissible in evidence when seeking to interpret the contract: see text to n. 81 below.

[38]   The judgment of Mr Justice Mocatta is unreported.

[39]   [1972] 1 WLR 840. Note that the decision was reached by a majority: Stephenson LJ dissented on the ground that, in his view, the word 'condition' had been used by the parties in its technical sense.

[40]   There was no appeal against the finding that Schuler was not entitled to terminate the contract pursuant to clause 11(a)(i).

18

of the contract on the ground of the failure by Wickman to comply with its obligations under clause 7(b) of the contract[41]. In English law, the entitlement of a contracting party to terminate further performance of the contract depends in part upon the nature of the term broken and in part on the consequences that follow from the breach. If the term broken is a 'condition' of the contract then any breach of the term, no matter how significant or insignificant, in principle gives the innocent party the right to terminate further performance of the contract[42]. An important feature of English contract law is that it gives to the parties the entitlement to classify the legal nature of the terms of their contract; that is to say, the parties can decide to classify as a condition a term which a court or arbitrator would not ordinarily decide was of sufficient importance to give rise to a right to terminate in the event of breach[43]. Where the term broken is not a condition, but an intermediate or an innominate term, then the entitlement of the innocent party to terminate further performance of the contract will depend principally upon the consequences of the breach[44]. Where the consequences of the breach are sufficiently serious, in the sense that the breach substantially deprives the innocent party of the performance which it was entitled to expect under the contract, then the innocent party will have the right to terminate further performance of the contract, but not otherwise.

Clause 7(b) of the contract stated that the obligation of Wickman to visit the six nominated customers on a weekly basis was a 'condition'. This being the case, one would ordinarily anticipate that an arbitrator or judge

---

41   It is interesting to note that the appeal was allowed at each stage of the proceedings except at the final stage before the House of Lords. The disagreement between the arbitrator, Mr Justice Mocatta and the Court of Appeal and the fact that the decisions of the Court of Appeal and House of Lords were both majority decisions demonstrate that the certainty claimed by English lawyers for their law of contract may not be as great as appears at first sight. While it is the case that the remedial entitlement of the parties is clear where the term broken is a condition, there may be considerable uncertainty or disagreement as to whether or not the term broken is in fact a condition. The present case demonstrates that the courts can and do disagree when deciding whether a term in a particular case is or is not a condition. To this extent, it cannot be said that the hallmark of the law is its clarity.

42   See, for example, E McKendrick *Contract Law: Text, Cases and Materials* (Oxford, 2003), pp. 923-939.

43   See, for example, *Lombard North Central plc v Butterworth* [1987] QB 527.

44   Hongkong Fir Shipping Co Ltd v Kawasaki Kisen Kaisha Ltd [1962] 2 QB 26, on which see further E McKendrick *Contract Law: Text, Cases and Materials* (Oxford, 2003), pp. 941-948.

would conclude that any breach would give to the innocent party the right to terminate further performance of the contract[45]. But the House of Lords concluded that Schuler was not entitled to terminate the contract because they decided that clause 7(b) was not a condition in the sense that any breach of the clause gave to Schuler the right to terminate further performance of the contract.

The case is generally cited in the textbooks for the proposition that the use by the parties of the word 'condition' does not mean that the word is necessarily a condition in the technical sense that any breach of the term gives rise to the right to terminate further performance of the contract[46]. The difficulty is that the word 'condition' is used in the law and by commercial parties in different senses[47]. The word 'condition' can, as we have seen, mean a term of the contract the breach of which gives to the innocent party the right to terminate further performance of the contract. But it can also be used in a more general sense, as in the case where a commercial party makes use of its own 'terms and conditions of business.' In such a case, the word 'conditions' is clearly not being used in its technical sense or as a term of art; rather, it is used in a generic sense to denote the terms in use by that party, whether that term in law amounts to a condition, a warranty[48] or an intermediate term. On the facts of *Schuler v Wickman* Lord Reid concluded that the use of the word 'condition' in clause 7(b) was an 'indication' and possibly a 'strong indication'[49] that the parties had used the word in order to describe a term, the breach of which gave rise to a right to terminate further performance of the contract. But

---

45   This was the view taken by Mr Justice Mocatta in the High Court and by Stephenson LJ in his dissenting judgment in the Court of Appeal. The reasoning of Stephenson LJ on this matter is to be found at pp. 858-862.

46   See, for example, Cheshire, Fifoot and Furmston's *Law of Contract* (London, Butterworths, 14th edn, 2001) p. 170, n. 17 (where the case is discussed in critical terms); G Treitel *The Law of Contract* (London, Sweet & Maxwell, 11th edn, 2003) p. 792; J Beatson *Anson's Law of Contract* (Oxford, 28th edn, 2002) p. 134 and R Halson *Contract Law* (London, Pearson, 2001) p. 435.

47   In his judgment in the Court of Appeal in *Wickman* Lord Denning identified three different meanings of the word 'condition': see [1972] 1 WLR 840, 849-851. See more generally G Treitel '"Conditions" and "Conditions Precedent"' (1990) 106 *Law Quarterly Review*, 185.

48   A warranty is a lesser, subsidiary term of the contract. Breach of a warranty gives rise to a right to claim damages but does not entitle the innocent party to terminate further performance of the contract.

49   [1974] AC 235, 251.

it was not conclusive and he held that, on the facts, the parties had not used the word 'condition' in its technical sense. There would appear to be three principal reasons which led the majority[50] to this conclusion.

The first was that the conclusion that clause 7(b) was a condition in the technical sense would lead to unreasonable results and, as Lord Reid observed,

> 'the more unreasonable the result the more unlikely it is that the parties can have intended it, and if they do intend it the more necessary it is that they shall make that intention abundantly clear'.[51]

What unreasonable results would flow from the conclusion that clause 7(b) was a condition in the technical sense? The answer was that the parties could not reasonably be supposed to have intended that a single breach of clause 7(b) would give to Schuler the right to terminate further performance of the contract. As Lord Reid observed, the contract required Wickman to make some 1,400 visits during the agreed life-time of the contract and, while the clause conferred upon Wickman a limited right to send an 'alternate representative', he concluded that the parties could not have intended that 'failure to make even one visit' would entitle Schuler 'to terminate the contract however blameless Wickman might be'[52]. The validity of this conclusion is, perhaps, open to question[53]. Indeed, Lord Wilberforce, the dissentient judge in the House of Lords, challenged the assumptions of the majority on this point. Thus he stated that

> 'to call the clause arbitrary, capricious or fantastic, or to introduce as a test of its validity the ubiquitous reasonable man....is to assume, contrary to the evidence, that both parties to this contract adopted a standard of easygoing tolerance rather than one of aggressive, insistent punctuality and efficiency'.[54]

---

50   Lord Wilberforce dissented.
51   [1974] AC 235, 251.
52   *Ibid.*
53   For conflicting views on the point see Cheshire, Fifoot and Furmston's *Law of Contract* (London, Butterworths, 14th edn, 2001) p. 170, n. 17 (where the case is criticised) and H Collins *The Law of Contract* (London, Butterworths, 4th edn, 2003) p. 360 (where a more benevolent approach is taken and, while it is noted that the interpretation of the majority 'may appear unconvincing' it is pointed out that it does have the merit that it reinserts 'the value of co-operation into the contract by forbidding reliance on the term as a pretext').
54   [1974] AC 235, 263.

Further he added that the effect of concluding that clause 7(b) was not a condition was to deprive Schuler 'of any remedy in respect of admitted and by no means minimal breaches'[55]. The proposition that the conclusion of the majority deprived Schuler of any remedy has to be read with some caution. Schuler would, of course, be entitled to a remedy in damages. But its entitlement to recover substantial damages would depend on its ability to prove that it had suffered loss as a result of the failure by Wickman to make the promised visits. Proof of loss may, however, have been a very difficult task. A failure to make a visit may not have resulted in a loss at all (in the sense that the party to be visited would not have made an order even had it received a visit at the specified time) or it may have resulted in the loss of a substantial order. Given that the consequences of a failure to make a visit were unpredictable, is it necessarily unreasonable to conclude that Schuler intended to use the sanction of termination in order to ensure that Wickman discharged its duties under the contract? It is suggested that it is not. Yet the effect of the conclusion of the majority was in fact to make it extremely difficult for Schuler to ensure that Wickman complied with its obligations under clause 7(b)[56]. Thus, standing alone, the proposition that clause 7(b) was not a condition because of the unreasonable consequences which would have been generated by this conclusion does not seem particularly persuasive. But the conclusion can be supported by the two other reasons that were relied upon by the majority.

The second reason was that the contract was badly drafted. Thus Lord Reid stated that the contract was 'so obscure that I can have no confidence that this is its true meaning'[57] but, for the reasons which he gave, he concluded that it was the 'preferable construction'. The fact that the contract was poorly drafted was no doubt a factor which helped to persuade the court that the parties had not used the word 'condition' in its technical sense. Had the agreement been drafted clearly and with the benefit of legal advice, it is suggested that the court would have been

---

55   *Ibid.*

56   What was Schuler to do in the event of a breach of clause 7(b)? A remedy in damages would not in all probability be attractive, given the problems of proving loss. Termination would only be possible via clause 11 but that would give to Wickman the entitlement to 'remedy' the breach. Given this entitlement, it would be very difficult for Schuler to ensure that Wickman complied strictly with its obligations under clause 7(b).

57   *Ibid.* at p. 252. See also p. 249 where he referred to the fact that the 'interrelation and consequences of the various provisions' of the agreement were 'so ill-thought out'.

more likely to conclude that the word 'condition' had been used in its technical sense. The point that is being made here is not that the quality of the drafting was a conclusive factor: it was not. It was simply a factor which was taken into account by the courts when deciding whether or not the word 'condition' had been used in its technical sense.

The third reason, and for present purposes the most interesting one, concerned the relationship between clause 7(b) and clause 11 of the agreement. The events which occurred potentially fell within the scope of both clause 7(b) and clause 11. If the breach by Wickman constituted a 'material breach' within the meaning of clause 11 then the response of Schuler should not have been to terminate the contract immediately but to give notice to Wickman in writing which required it to remedy the breach within 60 days of receiving the notice. The essential issue in the case can therefore be reduced to the following: did the parties intend the present case to be governed by clause 7(b) or by clause 11? The majority of the House of Lords concluded that it was governed by clause 11. Lord Reid rejected the submission, advanced on behalf of Schuler, that the case did not fall within the scope of clause 11 because the breach could not be 'remedied' given that the failures to make the promised visits were a matter of past, historical fact which could not be undone. In his opinion, the word 'remedy' could not be read in such a limited way. He concluded that the failure to make a single visit could be remedied by 'making arrangements to prevent a recurrence of that breach'[58]. Did this interpretation deprive clause 7(b) of all effect? Lord Reid concluded that it did not on the ground that the word 'condition' in clause 7(b) had the effect that 'any breach...however excusable', would be a 'material breach'[59] which

---

58   *Ibid.* at p. 250.

59   *Ibid.* at pp. 250-251. The arbitrator appeared to adopt a different view. His award has not been published and so it is not possible to be certain on this point. But Lord Denning records ([1972] 1 WLR 840, 849) that the arbitrator concluded that the word 'condition' indicated the 'importance attached by the parties to the stipulation so that it was a proper matter to consider whether there was a material breach within clause 11(a)(i).' On this view, a breach of clause 7(b) did not necessarily amount to a material breach; it was merely a factor to be taken into account when deciding whether or not there had been a material breach. That this was in fact the view of the arbitrator gains support from the fact that he found that, while there had been failures to visit the 6 named firms, these breaches were not material. On the view of Lord Reid, he should have found that the breaches were material. It would appear that Lord Morris (at p. 259) agreed with the reasoning of the arbitrator on this point.

would trigger the operation of clause 11. It is this point, concerning the relationship between the different terms of the contract, that is missed when insufficient attention is paid to the importance of the terms of the contract. Had clause 7(b) stood alone, it may well have been regarded as a condition in its technical sense. But, when viewed in the light of clause 11, the majority were persuaded that this was not the intention of the parties and that the function of clause 7(b) was, essentially, to assist in the definition of a 'material breach' for the purposes of clause 11. While this was probably not the intention of the representatives of Schuler who negotiated the contract with Wickman, the law is not concerned with the subjective intentions of the parties[60] but with their objective intention. The reality of the case is that the representatives of Schuler failed to spell out in express terms the relationship between clause 7(b) and clause 11(a)(i) and, faced with potentially overlapping clauses, the majority of the House of Lords chose, albeit with considerable hesitation, the construction which, in their view, led to the more reasonable result.

Seen in this light *Schuler v Wickman* does not stand for the proposition that it is dangerous to use the word 'condition' in a contract if the intention of the parties is to use the term in its technical sense. Rather it illustrates a much more limited proposition, namely that the courts may reach the conclusion that the word 'condition' has not been used in its technical sense where (i) the contract is badly drafted, (ii) it contains potentially overlapping clauses and (iii) unreasonable consequences may be said to flow from the conclusion that the word 'condition' was used in its technical sense. In this way *Schuler v Wickman* demonstrates the cardinal importance of paying careful attention to the terms of the contract and to the relationship between the various terms in the contract. Not only will such an examination assist in the identification of the scope of the legal rule that has been laid down in a particular case, it will also open the eyes

---

However Lord Simon (at p. 264) expressed his agreement with the reasoning of Lord Reid. Lord Kilbrandon did not express a clear view on this particular issue.

60   Although the arbitrator did admit evidence of the intention of the parties. Lord Denning records ([1972] 1 WLR 840, 849) that the arbitrator was aware of the fact that such evidence was not 'strictly admissible' but nevertheless 'allowed it de bene esse.' The evidence demonstrated that Schuler intended to use the word 'condition' in its technical sense but that that intention was not shared by Wickman and, further, that Wickman would not have signed the contract had they realised that the word had been used in its technical sense. The conflicting evidence of the parties was therefore not 'helpful'.

of students to the practical problems which can and do arise when drafting contracts. While it is not the function of law schools to teach drafting skills, it does not follow from this that we should be blind to them. A law school which requires its students to examine the rules of contract law but not the terms of contracts will produce students who have an inadequate understanding of the way in which commercial contracts operate in the modern world and a deficient understanding of the scope of the rule laid down in some of the leading cases.

.

II.   INTERPRETATION

The claim that the standard terms to be found in modern commercial contracts are of great significance both for legal practice and for legal education is an important one in terms of the current debate on the harmonisation of contract law. In particular, it suggests a rather different agenda for those involved in the process of harmonisation. Rather than focus on issues of legal doctrine, such as consideration, cause etc, greater attention ought to be given to the rules and principles applied by the courts when interpreting contractual documents. This is so for three reasons.

First, as has been noted, commercial parties generally have their own standard terms and conditions of business and the meaning of these terms is a matter of great significance to them. Second, these terms are often used not only for domestic transactions (that is to say, contracts between parties within the same jurisdiction) but for international or cross-border transactions. The use of standard terms in contracts between parties from different jurisdictions makes the development of a common understanding of these terms a matter of greater importance. If standard contract terms are interpreted in different ways in different jurisdictions or if the parties' understanding of these terms differs as between different jurisdictions, then greater difficulties are likely to arise when seeking to conclude an international transaction. Third, many contract disputes turn on the proper interpretation of the terms of the contract that has been concluded between the parties. That this is so can be illustrated by the fact that the most cited case in modern English contract law is *Investors Compensation Scheme v West Bromwich Building Society*[61], case in which Lord Hoffmann re-stated the principles to be applied by the courts when interpreting contractual documents. A common approach to the interpretation of contracts could play a significant role in terms of reducing disputes or making disputes easier to resolve.

The difficulty is that there are a number of obstacles that stand in the way of the development of a common approach to the interpretation

---

61   [1998] 1 WLR 896. The case is discussed in more detail below. A LEXIS search conducted on 14 October 2002 revealed that the case had been cited in over 180 cases. The case continues to be cited regularly in the courts. See further E McKendrick 'The Interpretation of Contracts: Lord Hoffmann's Re-Statement' in S Worthington (ed) *Commercial Law and Commercial Practice* (Hart, Oxford, 2003) p. 139.

of contractual documents. The principal obstacle is the differences that exist within national laws in Europe. These differences exist at a number of levels. The first relates to the aim of the interpretative process. In so far as its aim is to give effect to the intention of the parties, is their intention to be assessed objectively or subjectively? Is the aim of the court to identify the literal meaning of the words that have been used by the parties or to give effect to the commercial purpose of the transaction? If the courts are entitled to have regard both to the (literal) meaning of the words used and the commercial purpose of the transaction, what is the weight to be given to these different considerations? Should the literal meaning prevail over the commercial purpose (where the two are in conflict) or vice versa? The second difference relates to the range of materials that is admissible in evidence when interpreting a contractual document. Is the court entitled to have regard to pre-contractual negotiations and the conduct of the parties subsequent to the conclusion of the contract when seeking to ascertain the meaning of a contract term? The third difference relates to the powers of the court. Is the court entitled to re-write or adjust the contract in order to give effect to the intention of the parties or must it give effect to the contract as it stands, even in the case where the terms of the contract do not appear to coincide with the probable intention of the parties? If the courts do have a power to adjust the contract, what are the limits of this power?

Against this background, the prospect of the development of a common set of rules or principles for the interpretation of contractual documents appears slim. But there may be some cause for optimism. The Principles of European Contract Law may play an important role in bringing the different national systems closer together. Chapter 5 of the Principles is devoted to the interpretation of contracts. For our purposes the principal provisions are Articles 5:101 and 5:102. These Articles are in the following terms:

- 5:101: General Rules of Interpretation

    (1) A contract is to be interpreted according to the common intention of the parties even if this differs from the literal meaning of the words.

    (2) If it is established that one party intended the contract to have a particular meaning, and at the time of the conclusion of the contract the other party could not have been unaware of the first party's intention, the contract is to be interpreted in the way intended by the first party.

(3) If an intention cannot be established according to (1) or (2), the contract is to be interpreted according to the meaning that reasonable persons of the same kind as the parties would give to it in the same circumstances.

-     5:102: Relevant Circumstances

In interpreting a contract, regard shall be had, in particular, to:
(a) the circumstances in which it was concluded, including the preliminary negotiations;
(b) the conduct of the parties, even subsequent to the conclusion of the contract;
(c) the nature and purpose of the contract;
(d) the interpretation which has already been given to similar clauses by the parties and the practices they have established between themselves;
(e) the meaning commonly given to terms and expressions in the branch of activity concerned and the interpretation similar clauses may already have received;
(f) usages; and
(g) good faith and fair dealing.

It is not possible within the scope of this paper to compare these provisions with the rules that prevail within all the domestic legal systems in Europe. So I shall use English law as my comparator. I do so for two reasons. First, it is the legal system with which I am most familiar. Second, it may be that the most significant differences that exist between the Principles and a national European legal system are the differences that exist between the Principles and English law[62]. English law may therefore provide a good test case for the acceptability of the Principles.

It is necessary to provide a brief sketch of English law on the interpretation of contractual documents before comparing it with the Principles. It is probably fair to say that English law is generally associated with a literal approach to the interpretation of contractual documents. This traditional view was classically expressed by Lord Cozens-Hardy MR in *Lovell and Christmas Ltd v Wall*[63] when he stated that it is 'the duty of the court, which is presumed to understand the English language, to construe the document according to the ordinary grammatical meaning of the words used therein, and without reference to anything which has previously passed between the parties to it'[64]. But this traditional approach

---

62   See, for example, O Lando and H Beale (eds) *Principles of European Contract Law Parts I and II* (Kluwer, The Hague, 2000), pp. 290 and 293.
63   (1911) 104 LT 85.
64   *Ibid.* at p. 28.

29

has come under attack in recent years and it is clear that the English courts are no longer wedded to a literal approach to the interpretation of documents. As Lord Steyn observed in *Deutsche Genossenschaftsbank v Burnhope*[65]

'parallel to the shift during the last two decades from a literalist to a purposive approach to the construction of statutes there has been a movement from a strict or literal method of construction of commercial contracts towards an approach favouring a commercially sensible construction'.[66]

The principles applied by the English courts were recently re-stated by Lord Hoffmann in *Investors Compensation Scheme Ltd v West Bromwich Building Society*[67] in the following terms:

'I think I should preface my explanation of my reasons with some general remarks about the principles by which contractual documents are nowadays construed. I do not think that the fundamental change which has overtaken this branch of the law, particularly as a result of the speeches of Lord Wilberforce in *Prenn v Simmonds* [1971] 1 WLR 1381 at 1384-1386 and *Reardon Smith Line Ltd v Hansen-Tangen, Hansen-Tangen v Sanko Steamship Co* [1976] 1 WLR 989, is always sufficiently appreciated. The result has been, subject to one important exception, to assimilate the way in which such documents are interpreted by judges to the common sense principles by which any serious utterance would be interpreted in ordinary life. Almost all the old intellectual baggage of "legal" interpretation has been discarded. The principles may be summarised as follows.

(1) Interpretation is the ascertainment of the meaning which the document would convey to a reasonable person having all the background knowledge which would reasonably have been available to the parties in the situation in which they were at the time of the contract.

(2) The background was famously referred to by Lord Wilberforce as the "matrix of fact", but this phrase is, if anything, an understated description of what the background may include. Subject to the requirement that it should have been reasonably available to the parties and to the exception to be mentioned next, it includes absolutely anything which would have affected the way in which the language of the document would have been understood by a reasonable man.

---

65   [1995] 1 WLR 1580.
66   *Ibid.* at p. 1589. See also *Lord Napier and Ettrick v R F Kershaw Ltd* [1999] 1 WLR 756, 763; *Mannai Investment Co Ltd v Eagle Star Life Assurance Co Ltd* [1997] AC 749, 770 and *Total Gas Marketing Ltd v Arco British Ltd* [1998] 2 Lloyd's Rep 209, 221.
67   [1998] 1 WLR 896, 912-913.

(3) The law excludes from the admissible background the previous negotiations of the parties and their declarations of subjective intent. They are admissible only in an action for rectification. The law makes this distinction for reasons of practical policy and, in this respect only, legal interpretation differs from the way we would interpret utterances in ordinary life. The boundaries of this exception are in some respects unclear. But this is not the occasion on which to explore them.

(4) The meaning which a document (or any other utterance) would convey to a reasonable man is not the same thing as the meaning of its words. The meaning of words is a matter of dictionaries and grammars; the meaning of the document is what the parties using those words against the relevant background would reasonably have been understood to mean. The background may not merely enable the reasonable man to choose between the possible meanings of words which are ambiguous but even (as occasionally happens in ordinary life) to conclude that the parties must, for whatever reason, have used the wrong words or syntax (see *Mannai Investment Co Ltd v Eagle Star Life Assurance Co Ltd* [1997] 2 WLR 945).

(5) The "rule" that words should be given their "natural and ordinary meaning" reflects the commonsense proposition that we do not easily accept that people have made linguistic mistakes, particularly in formal documents. On the other hand, if one would nevertheless conclude from the background that something must have gone wrong with the language, the law does not require judges to attribute to the parties an intention which they plainly could not have had. Lord Diplock made this point more vigorously when he said in *Antaios Cia Naviera SA v Salen Rederierna AB, The Antaios* [1985] AC 191 at 201:

". . . if detailed semantic and syntactical analysis of words in a commercial contract is going to lead to a conclusion that flouts business common sense, it must be made to yield to business common sense".[68]

What differences exist between Lord Hoffmann's re-statement and Articles 5:101 and 5:102 of the Principles of European Contract Law? There are a number of potential differences. The first relates to the basic approach towards the interpretation of contractual documents. The emphasis in the Principles is upon the 'common intention of the parties', whereas Lord Hoffmann's re-statement has as its focus 'the meaning which the document would convey to a reasonable person'. This is not to suggest that Lord Hoffmann was unconcerned with the intention of the parties. His

---

68   [1998] 1 WLR 896, 912-913. He 'qualified' his second principle in *Bank of Credit and Commerce International v Ali* [2001] UKHL 8; [2002] 1 AC 251 at [39] when he said that the matrix of fact, while it had 'no conceptual limit', was limited to 'anything which a reasonable man would have regarded as *relevant*'.

fifth principle clearly demonstrates the significance of their intention and his unwillingness to impose on the parties a meaning other than that which they intended. But the impression is given that he attaches greater significance to the meaning of words or, more accurately, the meaning of documents than is the case with the Principles. This may be reflected in the fact that cases can be found in which the English courts have subjected contractual documents to careful textual analysis. The legitimacy of this careful textual evaluation may, however, be open to question. Second, the Principles expressly confer upon the court the entitlement to adopt a meaning of the words used other than their literal meaning where that is consistent with the 'common intention of the parties'. Lord Hoffmann's fifth principle is in similar vein but the extent to which it entitles the court to adjust or, more pejoratively, re-write the contract for the parties is a matter of debate. There may, on this issue, be a difference between courts in different jurisdictions in relation to their willingness to exercise such a power. Third, English law excludes from admissible evidence certain matters that are admissible under the Principles, namely pre-contractual or preliminary negotiations and the conduct of the parties subsequent to the making of the contract. These three issues will be considered briefly before concluding this section with a consideration of the extent to which it is possible to ensure that words and phrases in common use in commercial contracts are given the same meaning in different jurisdictions.

(a)   The meaning of documents and the intention of the parties

Lord Hoffmann's re-statement clearly does not require the courts to adopt a literal meaning of the words used by the parties. Indeed, his fourth and fifth principles expressly repudiate such a notion. Nevertheless, the aim of his re-statement is clearly to devise a set of principles which will assist the court in the identification of the meaning of the document in which the parties have chosen to enshrine their agreement. While it recognises that parties can and do make linguistic mistakes, it acknowledges that the inference of a mistake should not lightly be drawn. This being the case, the first task of the court is to examine the meaning of the words and phrases used by the parties in an effort to ascertain the meaning which the document would convey to a reasonable person having the background knowledge reasonably available to the contracting parties.

This process may require the court to engage in a careful analysis of the words which have been used by the parties. An example, albeit one which pre-dates *Investors Compensation Scheme,* is *Kleinwort Benson Ltd v Malaysia Mining Corporation Berhad*[69]. The claimants agreed to make available to a subsidiary company of the defendants a £10 million credit facility. The defendants refused to act as guarantors but they gave to the claimants a letter of comfort which stated that 'it is our policy to ensure that the business of [the subsidiary company] is at all times in a position to meet its liabilities to you under the above arrangements'. The subsidiary company ceased to trade after the collapse of the tin market at a time when its indebtedness to the claimants was £10 million. The defendants refused to honour their undertaking in the letter of comfort and so the claimants took proceedings against them, arguing that the defendants were in breach of contract in failing to pay. But the Court of Appeal held that the letter of comfort did not amount to a contractual promise by the defendants as to their future conduct. Therefore they were not liable to honour the debts of their subsidiary. It was held that the letter of comfort was simply a representation of fact as to the defendants' policy at the time at which the statement was made. The defendants did not promise that they would not change their policy for the future; they did not state that 'it is *and will at all times continue to be* our policy to ensure that the subsidiary will at all times be in a position to meet its liabilities to you'.

This insistence upon a careful examination of the words used by the parties has its critics. One of these critics is Rogers CJ in the Supreme Court of New South Wales who reached a very different conclusion in *Banque Brussels Lambert SA v Australian National Industries Ltd*[70]. The facts were similar to those in the *Kleinwort Benson* case. The relevant part of the letter of comfort stated:

> 'We take this opportunity to confirm that it is our practice to ensure that our affiliate [the borrower] will at all times be in a position to meet its financial obligations as they fall due. These financial obligations include repayment of all outstanding loans within thirty (30) days.'

---

69   [1989] 1 WLR 379.
70   [1989] 21 NSWLR 502.

Rogers CJ held that the letter of comfort was intended to be legally binding and that it amounted to a promise by the defendants that they would at all times ensure that the borrower was in a position to repay all loans made to it by the bank. He was critical of the 'minute textual analysis' employed by the Court of Appeal in *Kleinwort Benson* and concluded that 'it is inimical to the effective administration of justice in commercial disputes that a court should use a finely tuned linguistic fork'[71]. The approach of Rogers CJ has found some academic support. Thus one commentator stated that 'it is simply absurd to think that teams of lawyers and business people spend time and money drafting documents that express only moral obligations. It is even more absurd that they then act on these documents by entering into transactions worth millions of dollars'[72].

But the appropriateness of the Court of Appeal's 'finely tuned linguistic fork' must surely depend upon whether the parties to the contract intended that such an approach should be used in the interpretation of their contract. It is likely that the letter of comfort in both cases was the subject of intense negotiations between the parties. In both cases the parent company refused to provide the bank with a guarantee and instead offered the bank such comfort as they could derive from the letter drawn up on behalf of the parent company. In these circumstances the precise content of the letter of comfort is crucial. A lawyer drafting a letter of comfort on behalf of a bank would (or should) be alive to the difference between a statement 'it is our practice' and a statement that 'it is and will at all times continue to be our practice'. The former is a representation as to the parent company's current intention, whereas the latter has a future component and is open to the construction that it constitutes a promise by the parent company not to change its policy. In this respect it is suggested that the approach of Rogers CJ amounts to a disservice to the lawyers responsible for drafting the letter of comfort on the basis that it appears to transform a representation of current intention into a promise which bound the defendant for the future.

What would be the result of applying the Principles of European Contract Law to the facts of *Kleinwort Benson*? No clear answer can be given to this question in the absence of any authority on point. The answer in terms of Article 5:101 would presumably depend on the 'common inten-

---

71   *Ibid.* at p. 524.
72   Tyree 'Southern Comfort' (1989) 2 *Journal of Contract Law* 279, 282.

tion of the parties'. The difficulty is that the parties in *Kleinwort Benson* may not have had a 'common intention': the claimants wanted a guarantee, but the defendants refused to give them one. Further, the meaning of the letter of comfort was disputed by the parties. In the absence of a 'common intention' it would be necessary to revert to Article 5:101(3), but the meaning of that provision is less than clear. How would 'reasonable persons of the same kind as the parties' understand the letter of comfort? The answer will presumably depend on whether these reasonable people are represented by the Court of Appeal in *Kleinwort Benson* or by Rogers CJ in *Banque Brussels Lambert*. Much will therefore depend on the judge's view of the appropriateness of a 'finely tuned linguistic fork'. This is an issue on which judges may disagree within any single jurisdiction. It may therefore be unduly optimistic to expect a uniform answer to this particular question. Much may depend on the commercial context of the transaction. A document which has been drawn up by lawyers acting for commercial parties may be interpreted more literally (on the basis that the parties can be presumed to have chosen their words carefully) than a contract drawn up by businessmen who have not had access to legal advice and who concluded the agreement in an informal context[73]. However, practitioners working within a jurisdiction will want to know the meaning to be given to the words 'it is our policy to ensure....' because the approach taken by the judiciary will have a very significant impact on the approach taken towards the drafting of letters of comfort. In this sense, practitioners look for a consistent approach from the courts so that they can predict with some confidence the likely judicial approach to the interpretation of particular words or phrases inserted into a contract.

While this expectation is legitimate for purely domestic transactions, it may lose some of its validity when applied to international transactions. The solicitor from New South Wales who advises on a letter of comfort given by a UK parent company in favour of an Australian bank may have a very different view of the true meaning of the letter of comfort from the English lawyer acting for the UK parent company. The existence of a choice of law clause may, however, alert the respective lawyers to the

---

73 There are some signs of this in the English authorities. The courts seem to attach more importance to the natural and ordinary meaning of the document in cases involving formal documents drawn up by lawyers (particularly in the context of taxation and trusts): see, for example, *Breadner v Granville-Grossman* [2001] Ch 523 at [36].

approach that is likely to be taken to the interpretation of the letter. Thus, in the event that it is governed by English law, the letter will be interpreted in accordance with English principles and the New South Wales lawyer ought to take advice from an English lawyer on the true meaning and effect of the letter. There are two objections to this process. First, it adds to the cost of the transaction because it requires the Australian lawyer to take and pay for additional advice. Second, it might not in fact occur to the New South Wales lawyer to take this precaution. On the facts of this particular case the New South Wales lawyer should, in fact, be aware of the difference between the law of New South Wales and English law because *Banque Brussels Lambert* will tell him or her that the law in the two jurisdictions does diverge. But the objection will hold good in other cases. Lawyers cannot be expected to be familiar with all of the applicable rules in other jurisdictions, nor to take advice from foreign lawyers on each and every transaction that is governed by a foreign law. Account must also be taken of the case where there is no choice of law. This would appear to have been the case in *Kleinwort Benson* in the sense that there does not appear to have been any mention of a governing law in the letter of comfort issued on behalf of the defendants. In the case where there is no choice of law, how is the practitioner acting for a parent company to know how to draft a letter of comfort which provides the bank with an assurance as to the present intention of the parent company but does not commit the parent company in relation to its future policy? One method might be to set this out in full so that the letter of comfort includes a statement to the following effect:

> 'This letter reflects the current practice of [the parent company] but does not amount to a promise that this practice will be maintained in the future.'

The virtue of such a sentence is that it makes the limited nature of the undertaking explicit. The objection to the *Kleinwort Benson* case may be that its restricted scope was not stated with sufficient clarity; in particular, its limits may not have been apparent to a party to an international transaction whose first language was not English.

My aim in raising this issue is not to provide a definitive answer to the question of the meaning to be given to letters of comfort but to point out the importance of the answer to the question and the advantages that can be obtained if the same answer is given in different jurisdictions. If different answers are given in different jurisdictions lawyers who are a-ware of the different responses will have to adapt their standard form documentation in order to reflect the local approach to the interpretation of letters of comfort, while lawyers who are unaware of differences will find that, from time to time, the letter of comfort will be given a very different meaning from that which they perhaps intended. From this it can be seen that, in so far as the Principles aim to produce a uniform approach to the interpretation of contracts, they perform a useful function. The problem with the Principles is that they do not presently provide practitioners with the guidance which they require when drafting contracts. The factors listed in Article 5:102 are not objectionable in themselves (with the possible exception of 'good faith and fair dealing') but they are stated at a high level of generality and so do not provide a clear-cut answer to the problem raised on the facts of *Kleinwort Benson*. More has to be done in terms of formulating a common approach to issues of interpretation if the legitimate demands of commercial practice are to be met.

(b)   Commercial construction and re-writing the contract

A second issue, which is closely related to the first issue, relates to the powers of the courts in the interpretative process. In particular, does the court have the power to re-write or adjust the contract in order to give effect to what it perceives to be the common intention of the parties? The Principles provide a clear answer to this question: Article 5:101(1) empowers the court to depart from the literal meaning of the words chosen in order to give effect to the intention of the parties. English law is less clear-cut. Traditionally, the power of the courts to depart from the meaning of the words used by the parties was limited to the remedy of rectification but that remedy is only available within narrow limits[74]. Lord Hoffmann's re-statement offers the prospect of a more liberal approach in so far as his fourth and fifth principles entitle the courts, in certain circumstances, to depart from the literal meaning of the words used without resorting to the remedy of rectification. The extent of the courts' willingness to make use of the fourth and fifth principles is presently unclear. In particular, it

---

74   On which see E McKendrick *Contract Law: Text, Cases and Materials* (Oxford, 2003), pp. 616-621 and see footnote 86 below.

would appear that the courts are struggling[75] to find the dividing line between the adoption of a 'commercial construction' (which is legitimate) and judicial re-writing of the contract (which is illegitimate). The point may be a not unimportant one in practice. The speed with which transactions of huge value are currently concluded can have the consequence that the written terms of the deal contain some rough edges and the relationship between some of the terms can be distinctly murky. The extent to which the courts can smooth over the rough edges and iron out any apparent inconsistency between contract terms is not entirely clear. Cases can be found in which the courts have made allowances for the 'vicissitudes of drafting'[76] in order to give effect to the 'general aim'[77] of the contract. Similarly, it has been stated that the court may 'require what appear to be errors or inadequacies in the choice of language to yield to [the intention of the parties] and be understood as saying what (in the light of that purpose) that language must reasonably be understood to have been intended to mean'[78]. Not all judges are content with this process. In *Investors Compensation Scheme* Lord Lloyd dissented on the basis that the majority had crossed the line between legitimate purposive interpretation and illegitimate creative interpretation[79]. Yet it could be said that the change that has taken place in English law is more apparent than real. As *Schuler v Wickman* demonstrates, the courts have always been unwilling to adopt a construction that leads to a very unreasonable result. Nevertheless, the (perception of) change has had an unsettling effect on English law, in particular the proposition that there need no longer be an ambiguity in the contract before the court can resort to the surrounding circumstances or adopt a secondary or even unnatural interpretation of the words used[80].

---

75   See, for example, *Sinochem International Oil (London) Co Ltd v Mobil Sales and Supply Corporation* [2000] 1 Lloyd's Rep 339, 340 per Mance LJ.

76   *Ibid.* at p. 345. However it should be noted that Mance LJ stated (at p. 345) that the case involved a 'one-off contract'. Given that the issue was specific to the parties before the court, the interests of certainty probably did not weigh so heavily with the court, given the extremely limited impact of the decision.

77   *Ibid.*

78   *Don King Productions Ltd v Warren* [1998] 2 All ER 608, 624, cited with approval by Morritt LJ in the Court of Appeal, [1999] 2 All ER 218, 229-230.

79   [1998] 1 WLR 898, 904.

80   *Westminster City Council v National Asylum Support Service* [2002] UKHL 38 at [5].

The fear of many English practitioners is that a further liberalisation of the process will give rise to unacceptable uncertainty. This links back to the earlier discussion of the *Kleinwort Benson* case and the expectations which practitioners have of the courts. If the function of the courts is simply to give effect to the literal meaning of the words used by the parties then the role of the judge is a limited one. Lord Hoffmann has expanded the role of the English judge as a result of his emphasis, in his fourth and fifth principles, on the meaning of the document rather than the meaning of its words. This shift in emphasis enables judges to conclude that 'something has gone wrong with the language' and to give primacy to the intention of the parties over the natural meaning of the words in which they have chosen to enshrine their agreement. This is not in itself objectionable but it does give rise to concern to the extent that a party to a contract who discovers that the contract has turned out to be a bad bargain may attempt to escape from its plight by submitting that the agreement does not mean what it appears to mean and that it should be given some other construction which is more favourable to its position. This concern may be misplaced in so far as Lord Hoffmann expressly stated that the courts will not 'easily accept that people have made linguistic mistakes, particularly in formal documents'. But the *mere possibility* that a judge may conclude that a mistake has been made or that the parties have used words in an unnatural sense can generate uncertainty over the outcome of litigation where the parties are in dispute as to the meaning of a term or terms of a contract. The conferral on the judges of greater power to adjust or adapt the contract will only serve to generate further uncertainty.

It may be said that these concerns are unwarranted and that they reflect an undue emphasis on the supposed virtues of certainty. This may be true. But the issue is not without significance in terms of the approach to be taken towards the drafting of contracts. If the expectation of the practitioner is that the judge will give effect to the natural meaning of the words used in the contract and will depart from that meaning only in truly exceptional cases, the practitioner can predict the outcome of litigation with a degree of confidence and he or she also knows that great care must be taken when drafting the contract because the judge will not adjust the contract in the event that the parties have expressed their agreement in infelicitous terms. On the other hand, a power to adjust the contract may, at least initially, make the outcome of litigation harder to predict (because of the uncertainty as to whether or not the judge will exercise the power to adjust or adapt the contract) and it may induce greater laxity in the drafting process because the judge can be relied upon to rectify or undo any inadequacies in the contract itself. My point here is not to make a case for one approach being preferable to the other but rather to demonstrate that those responsible for drafting contracts do need to know the approach that will be taken by the courts when interpreting the contract because that approach will have an impact on the way in which the contract is drafted. A judge who is willing to make allowances for the 'vicissitudes of drafting' will not demand the precision of language required by a judge who makes no such allowance. These difficulties are compounded when judges in different systems adopt divergent approaches because the person responsible for drafting the contract must then adapt his or her style in order to reflect the different national approaches to interpretation. In such a situation the prospect of being able to use the same standard terms in different jurisdictions simply evaporates.

(c)   Pre-contractual negotiations

The third point relates to the range of materials that can be taken into account by the court when interpreting contractual documents. Lord Hoffmann's third principle is clearly more restrictive than Article 5:102(a) of the Principles in so far as the latter provides that the previous negotiations of the parties are not generally admissible in evidence. A similar point can be made in relation to the conduct of the parties subsequent to the making of the contract. Such evidence is generally inadmissible in England[81] but is expressly declared to be admissible in Article 5:102(b) of the Principles. Here I shall take pre-contractual negotiations as my example. Why does English law exclude pre-contractual negotiations from the interpretative process when they are admissible in evidence in most jurisdictions on the continent of Europe? The first possible reason is that the test to be applied when seeking to ascertain the intention of the parties is objective and not subjective. The court should not therefore concern itself with subjective statements by either party as to the meaning to be ascribed to a particular term. The law does not wish to encourage parties to make self-serving statements in the course of negotiations and then produce them in evidence when a dispute breaks out in relation to

---

81   *Schuler AG v Wickman Machine Tool Sales* [1974] AC 235.

the meaning of that particular term. The more objective stance adopted by the English courts in comparison with their continental counterparts may help to explain the exclusion of pre-contractual negotiations. But this is at best a partial explanation because the law excludes not simply the parties' statements about their subjective intent but objective evidence in the form of previous drafts. Secondly, the English courts have objected to the admissibility of pre-contractual negotiations on the basis that this evidence is not 'helpful'[82] because the task of the court is to decide 'what the final contract means'[83] and not to speculate as to the reasons which led to changes being made as between the various drafts. Again, this is not a conclusive argument because it relates to the helpfulness, or the weight, of the evidence and not to its admissibility. The fact that evidence of pre-contractual negotiations is 'unhelpful' in some cases, perhaps the majority of cases, does not mean that it should be held to be inadmissible in the cases where it is helpful. Third, it may be that evidence of pre-contractual negotiations is inadmissible because it would add to the already very high cost of litigation in England without producing corresponding benefits. Judges in England have already expressed concern that one effect of Lord Hoffmann's re-statement, in particular his second principle, may be to add to the already considerable cost of litigation in England[84]. To add still further to that cost by admitting evidence of pre-contractual negotiations may prove to be a step too far for the English judiciary and thus far they have not taken the step. The fact that the cost of litigation in England is significantly higher than the cost of litigation on the continent of Europe may help to explain why it is that pre-contractual negotiations are excluded in England but not elsewhere.

However, it may be that the differences between English law and the Principles are over-stated. The exclusion of pre-contractual negotiations in English law is not absolute. First, where there is an ambiguity in the final written document, evidence of pre-contractual negotiations may be admissible to show that the parties had attached a particular meaning

---

82   *Canterbury Golf International Ltd v Yoshimoto* [2002] UKPC 40 at [28].
83   *Ibid.*
84   See, for example, *National Bank of Sharjah v Dellborg*, Unreported, Court of Appeal, 9 July 1997; *Scottish Power plc v Britoil (Exploration) Ltd, The Times*, 2 December 1997 and *NLA Group Ltd v Bowers* [1999] 1 Lloyd's Rep 109. The issue is discussed in more detail by E McKendrick (n. 61 above) pp. 144-147.

to the ambiguous phrase[85]. Second, as Lord Hoffmann acknowledged, pre-contractual negotiations are admissible in an action for rectification[86]. Third, it would appear that evidence of the background and of the object and genesis of the transaction is admissible but that evidence of the parties' previous negotiating positions is not[87]. This distinction is not an easy one to draw. As Judge MacDuff QC stated in *Sykes v Pannell Kerr Forster*

> 'there is...a very fine borderline between the admissible and the inadmissible. One may look at the facts and circumstances surrounding the negotiation and that about which the parties were negotiating, but not at what the parties said during negotiations nor at previous drafts. The rationale, at least in part, appears to be a wish on the part of the courts to encourage open negotiations and to discourage the creation of self-serving documents or utterances.'[88]

Given these exceptions and the difficulties which the judges have experienced in distinguishing in this context between evidence which is admissible and evidence which is not[89], will English law maintain its current

---

85   *The Karen Oltman* [1976] 2 Lloyd's Rep 708.
86   Rectification is a remedy which is concerned with defects, not in the making, but in the recording of the contract. Thus it is a process whereby a document, the meaning of which has already been ascertained, is rectified so that it gives effect to the intention of the parties. This exception is of some importance in practice because one of the reasons sometimes given for pleading rectification is to render evidence of pre-contractual negotiations admissible. Of course this can only be done where there is a plausible basis for asking for rectification. The pre-contractual negotiations are only admissible in the rectification proceedings. The judge should disregard the evidence when considering any submissions made by the parties on the interpretation of the contract, but the party asking for rectification nevertheless hopes that the pre-contractual negotiations, once admitted into evidence, will influence the judge in reaching his or her conclusion on the proper interpretation of the contract, even though, for obvious reasons, no express reliance is placed by the judge on these negotiations.
87   *Gehe AG v NBTY Inc,* Unreported, QBD, 30 July 1999, cf *The Management Corporation Strata Title Plan No 193 v Liang Huat Aluminium Ltd* [2001] BLR 351.
88   Unreported, QBD, 30 March 2001. See also *Bank of Scotland v Dunedin Property Investment Co Ltd* 1998 SC 657 (a Scottish case) where Lord President Rodger stated that the rationale behind the exclusionary rule 'shows...that it has no application when the evidence of the parties' discussions is being considered, not in order to provide a gloss on the terms of the contract, but rather to establish the parties' knowledge of the circumstances with reference to which they used the words in the contract.'
89   See, for example, *Gould v BG Transco Ltd,* Unreported, Chancery Division, 10 August 2001; *The Tychy (No. 2)* [2001] EWCA Civ 1198; [2001] 2 Lloyd's Rep 403; *Biggin Hill Airport Ltd v Bromley London Borough Council, The Times,* 9 January 2000; *Gehe AG v*

stance? It is suggested that it will not. Now that the English courts give more weight to the adoption of an approach which seeks to give a commercially sensible construction to the clause in dispute, the justification for excluding pre-contractual negotiations from evidence appears suspect. Pre-contractual negotiations can provide very good evidence of the issue that is at stake between the parties and thus can be of direct assistance in terms of ascertaining the commercial purpose which the parties had in mind when entering into the contract. This being the case, evidence of pre-contractual negotiations should be admissible in evidence unless that evidence relates to the subjective state of mind of the negotiating parties. This is not to say that a great deal of weight should necessarily be given to evidence of pre-contractual negotiations. The weight will very much depend upon the facts of the case. But in principle evidence of pre-contractual negotiations should be admitted, even if, in many cases, it ultimately proves to be 'unhelpful'. In this respect the Principles of European Contract Law may have a role to play in terms of persuading the English judges to abandon their exclusionary rule and thereby bring English law into line with the approach adopted in most jurisdictions on the continent of Europe. In this respect at least we may soon see a gradual convergence of the rules applied by the courts when seeking to interpret disputed contract terms.

(d)   A common meaning for common terms

However, we are still a long way from the adoption of a common European set of rules or principles that can be applied when interpreting contractual documents. This being the case, contracting parties cannot safely assume that the meaning given to their boilerplate clauses will be the same in each jurisdiction in Europe. Thus words and phrases that are in common use in commercial contracts in Europe (such as 'force majeure', 'indirect or consequential loss' and 'material breach') may be given different meanings in different European jurisdictions. What can be done to reduce these differences of approach and to encourage the production of standard form clauses which are given the same meaning in different European jurisdictions? One answer may lie in the development of a

---

NBTY Inc, Unreported, QBD, 30 July 1999 and *Demolition Services Ltd v Castle Vale Housing Action Trust*, [1999] 79 Con LR 55.

'common frame of reference' as proposed by the European Commission in its Action Plan on European Contract Law[90]. While the exact meaning of the phrase 'common frame of reference' may be said to be elusive, one meaning that can be given to the phrase is that a common terminology should be developed for words and phrases that are in frequent use in commercial contracts within Europe. That such a development falls within the scope of the Action Plan is supported by the fact that the Commission proposed the elaboration and promotion of 'EU-wide standard contract terms'[91]. The Commission proposes to facilitate the exchange of information on existing initiatives which aim to develop such standard terms and conditions and to offer guidelines on their use.

This is clearly a step in the right direction and, as such, it should be applauded. But it may be necessary to take more radical steps. Three principal points can be made here. The first is that the Action Plan is less than convincing in its handling of standard contract terms. It states that standard contract terms are typically drawn up by parties from a single Member State and 'may therefore be less adapted to the particular needs of cross-border transactions'[92]. While it is true that many contract terms have been developed within a single jurisdiction (and indeed this is a significant source of the problems identified in this lecture), it is also true that there have been a number of important international attempts to draft standard contract terms. The Action Plan acknowledges this but refers only to the work of Orgalime, 'a European trade association in the metal-working, mechanical and electrical engineering sector [which] has developed General Conditions, Model Forms and Guides to provide practical assistance for companies when they draw up different types of contracts which are commonly used in international trade in the sectors covered'[93]. Rather curiously, no reference is made to the standard trade terms promulgated by institutions such as the International Chamber of Commerce. This is an important omission. If a serious attempt is to be made to secure a common understanding of standard contract terms, then the study must embrace the work of the important international organisations whose work to date has had a significant impact on the drafting of standard

---

90   COM(2003) 68 final, OJ 2003 C63/01.
91   *Ibid.* paras 81-88.
92   *Ibid.* para 84.
93   *Ibid.* footnote 59, para. 84.

44

contract terms. Second, the Action Plan could have said more about the standard terms to be found in modern commercial contracts. It does discuss the difficulties that arise when seeking to rely upon retention of title clauses but the discussion is very much focused on the impact of rules of law on the efficacy of these clauses. The burden of this lecture is to argue that boilerplate clauses are important in and of themselves and that we ought to focus to a greater extent on the identification of the meaning to be given to these clauses. It is therefore important to identify words and phrases (such as 'force majeure' and 'indirect or consequential loss') which are a recipe for confusion in cross-border transactions. The Action Plan largely fails to identify such clauses. Thirdly, the Action Plan has very little to say on the interpretation of contracts. It does state that the common frame of reference can be expected to contain 'general rules on....interpretation of contracts' but a firmer link must be established between the elaboration of standard contract terms and their interpretation. To put the point bluntly, there is little point in drawing up such standard terms if they are to be interpreted in different ways in different Member States. While the Action Plan is undoubtedly a step in the right direction there is more to be done. There ought to be a clearer focus on standard contract terms that are to be found in modern commercial contracts and on the principles to be applied when interpreting such clauses. The development of a common set of standard contract terms and the production of a common interpretation of these clauses would be a significant step forward in the harmonisation process and in terms of facilitating trade within Europe.

III.   REGULATION AND MANDATORY RULES

The final part of this lecture deals, albeit briefly, with mandatory rules. This is a topic of some complexity, especially in relation to private international law[94]. It is not my intention to enter into these difficult waters at this point. My aim here is much simpler, namely to highlight the difficulties which are created for those responsible for drafting boilerplate clauses by rules of law that cannot be derogated from by contract. In making this point I do not wish to suggest that nation states should immediately abandon all mandatory rules of contract law. These rules should continue to exist where they serve a useful purpose. But where their existence is attributable to the dead-hand of history rather than the needs of the modern world they should be abandoned. Further, where they continue to exist, they should be harmonised to the fullest extent possible so that lawyers in different jurisdictions are not taken by surprise by mandatory rules of which they were wholly unaware.

That mandatory rules can cause difficulties in practice is demonstrated by the European Commission in its Action Plan where it is pointed out that 'some commentators' stressed that 'the main problems in the contract law area result from provisions which restrict contractual freedom'[95]. While these problems can be avoided in part by resort to a choice of law clause, they cannot be eliminated[96]. The Commission point out some of the problem areas, namely requirements of form which are mandatory for certain contracts[97], rules relating to the incorporation of terms into a contract[98], and rules which regulate the fairness of standard form contracts[99]. They conclude that this type of control 'creates uncertainty for businesses that use standard terms....hampers the use of ready made

---

94   See generally Dicey and Morris *The Conflict of Laws* (13th edn, 2000, London, Sweet & Maxwell) paras 32R-128-32-150.

95   See n. 90 above at para 26.

96   This is most obviously so where the mandatory rules are to be found in the applicable law. But mandatory rules can override choice of law clauses in different ways. Thus the mandatory laws of the forum state (Article 7(2) of the Rome Convention on the Law Applicable to Contractual Obligations) and of a third country which has a close connection with the contract (Article 7(1) of the Rome Convention) may override the choice of law clause.

97   See n. 90 above at para 35.

98   *Ibid.* para 36.

99   *Ibid.* para 37.

standard contracts that were actually created to facilitate cross-border transactions and intended for use in any legal system' and makes it 'necessary to use different standard contracts in different Member States, which in turn makes it impossible to use the same business model for the whole European market'[100]. These criticisms should, however, be seen in their context. Mandatory rules of law are relatively few in the context of commercial contract law (that is to say, contracts concluded between two parties who are both acting in the course of their business[101]). Mandatory rules of law are much more likely to be encountered in the context of contracts concluded between a consumer and a party acting in the course of a business. These mandatory rules principally exist in order to protect consumers from exploitation and it is highly unlikely that these rules will disappear (indeed it would be undesirable if they did). In terms of the future role of mandatory rules of law, it is suggested that a distinction can usefully be drawn between four different types of contract.

The first consists of consumer contracts, by which I mean to refer to contracts concluded between a party[102] who is acting in the course of a business and a person who is not[103]. Such contracts are already the subject of a number of mandatory rules, particularly where the contract term has not been individually negotiated. It would be neither possible nor desirable to seek to eliminate all of these mandatory rules. This being the case, the aim should be to harmonise as far as possible the content of these mandatory rules across Europe. In this respect, considerable progress has been made as a result of the Directive on Unfair Terms in Consumer Contracts[104] which provides a framework for the regulation of standard terms in consumer contracts. The continued harmonisation of these mandatory rules is likely to become more urgent as a result of the growth in the use of the internet which will involve consumers in more transactions with businesses which cross national borders.

---

100   *Ibid.* para 38.
101   Although a difficulty can arise from the fact that the phrase 'acting in the course of a business' does not have a common meaning and therefore is given different meanings within the different jurisdictions in Europe.
102   A 'party' includes a company for this purpose.
103   In other words, I do not intend in this paper to deal with contracts concluded between two consumers, that is to say, neither party is acting in the course of a business.
104   Law Commission Consultation Paper No 166; Scottish Law Commission Discussion Paper No 119 *Unfair Terms in Contracts: A Joint Consultation Paper* (2002).

The second category consists of contracts concluded between two parties acting in the course of a business and the contract is concluded on the standard terms and conditions of one of the parties to the transaction. In the United Kingdom the Law Commission and the Scottish Law Commission have recently provisionally proposed the extension of court controls over terms in business-to-business contracts which have not been individually negotiated[105]. These provisional proposals have aroused some controversy on the ground that they are said by some to be an unwarranted intrusion into freedom of contract and that they will give rise to an unacceptable amount of uncertainty in commercial transactions. It is not possible within the scope of this lecture to resolve this particular issue. It suffices to point out that such controls currently fall within the domain of national law and that the extent of the regulation of standard contract terms in business contracts varies as between the different Member States in Europe. In relation to such contracts, it is suggested that the default rule ought to be that they should not be subject to mandatory rules of law. Freedom of contract ought to be the starting point and the law should only take away that freedom where clear, countervailing reasons exist. It would be helpful if these 'clear, countervailing reasons' could be the same in all European States.

The third category consists of contracts concluded between two parties acting in the course of a business but this time the contract is not concluded on the standard terms and conditions of one of the parties to the transaction. Given that this type of contract has the appearance of a freely negotiated transaction (in the sense that neither party was able to impose its own standard terms and conditions on the other), there is a case for saying that these contracts should not be subject to the same controls as are applicable to terms in business to business contracts which have not been individually negotiated. This is currently the general position in the UK and the Law Commissions have not proposed any change in this respect. Yet this category may be thought to be troublesome. It is not always entirely easy to distinguish between a contract (or a contract term) which has been individually negotiated and one which has not[106]. For

---

105 Law Commission Consultation Paper No 166; Scottish Law Commission Discussion Paper No 119 *Unfair Terms in Contracts: A Joint Consultation Paper* (2002).

106 Thus the phrase 'deals...on the other's written standard terms of business' in section 3(1) of the Unfair Contract Terms Act 1977 has given rise to some interpretative difficulties in the courts.

example, what is to be done in the case of standard terms and conditions which are the subject of some negotiation between the parties but these negotiations do not result in any changes to the standard terms and conditions? Or the case where there have been some changes but no changes have been made to the term which is now in issue between the parties? The fact that we have difficulty in assigning cases to one category or the other might suggest that a distinction between this category and the previous category is not worth drawing. Commercial parties frequently use their own standard terms and conditions as the starting point in negotiations and, if we cannot decide whether standard terms that have been the subject of meaningful negotiation between the parties fall into this category or the previous one, then the distinction is probably not worth drawing. In any event, the default rule ought to be that such contracts should not be subject to mandatory rules of law and, as was the case with our second category, that rule should only be displaced in exceptional circumstances.

The final category consists of contracts concluded between two parties acting in the course of a business and neither party has a connection with the chosen jurisdiction except the existence of a choice of law clause in their contract. Should contracting parties be given the freedom to evade the application of mandatory rules of one nation state by choosing the law of another nation state? This is a difficult question. English law currently does allow such contracting parties the possibility to exempt themselves from some of the regulatory controls that would otherwise be applicable[107]. Thus section 27(1) of the Unfair Contract Terms Act 1977 states that, where the law applicable to a contract is the law of any part of the United Kingdom only by virtue of the choice of the parties to the contract, sections 2-7 of the Act (which, broadly speaking, regulate exclusion and limitation of liability for breach of contract and for negligence) do not operate as part of the law applicable to the contract. The effect of this provision is to allow foreign parties to choose English law shorn of the

---

107   But note that the regulatory controls may not be applicable. Important in this context is section 26 of the Unfair Contract Terms Act 1977 which, broadly speaking, provides that the limits provided by the Act on the extent to which a person may exclude or restrict liability by reference to a contract term do not apply to liability arising under an international supply contract. The effect of this provision is to take many cross-border transactions outside the scope of the regulatory regime set up under the Act.

regulatory controls to be found in the Act. Here we see a legal system operating as a market, seeking to obtain business by making itself as attractive as possible to potential users from other jurisdictions. The desirability of this provision is, however, open to question. In any event, it may not give the parties the freedom that they cherish because, in the case where the parties choose English law in order to avoid the mandatory rules of another European legal system with which the contract is otherwise closely connected, the English courts may nevertheless be required to apply the mandatory rules of law of the otherwise applicable law[108]. This reveals the other side of the coin, namely the attempt by nation states to regulate the evasion of regulatory controls by the use of choice of law clauses. The Unfair Contract Terms Act itself contains provisions which seek to regulate attempts to evade the application of the Act by a choice of law clause. Thus section 27(2) of the Act provides that the controls contained in the Act cannot be evaded by a choice of a law outside the United Kingdom as the governing law if it appears, firstly, that the choice of law was imposed wholly or mainly to enable the party imposing it to evade the operation of the Act or, secondly, where one of the parties dealt as a consumer, was then habitually resident in the United Kingdom and the essential steps for the making of the contract were taken in the United Kingdom. The latter exception is an important provision in terms of consumer protection. The scope of the first exception is more problematic because it raises some difficult issues of interpretation[109]. But the essence of section 27 is clear. While the legislators were willing in principle to allow parties to contract into English law without thereby subjecting themselves to the regulatory control to be found in the Act, they were not willing to give contracting parties the unfettered right to use a choice of law clause as a device to evade that regulatory control where English law would otherwise be applicable to the contract. In other words, the policy is to allow the choice of law market to operate but to regulate its excesses. A better approach would be to reduce the significance of the market by seeking to harmonise the mandatory rules of contract law within Europe. If this can be done not only will those responsible for drafting contracts know of the existence of these mandatory rules but the temptation to seek

---

108   Pursuant to Article 3(3) of the Rome Convention on the Law Applicable to Contractual Obligations.

109   On which see *Benjamin's Sale of Goods* (6th edn, 2002) paras 25-094 - 25-100.

to avoid their application by the choice of the law of another European State will also be removed[110].

Of course the range of mandatory rules is not confined to rules which seek to regulate the fairness of standard contract terms. I have used these rules simply as an example. My point is that mandatory rules can and do act as a barrier to the use of boiler-plate clauses in cross-border transactions. This being the case, steps should be taken to harmonise mandatory rules in Europe, not only in the case of consumer contracts but also in the case of business-to-business contracts in those (rare) cases where it is thought appropriate to apply mandatory rules.

---

110   Of course, it will still be necessary to regulate attempts to evade the operation of mandatory rules by the choice of law clause which selects as the law applicable to the contract the law of a non-European State.

CONCLUSION

In this lecture I have endeavoured to do four things. The first is to demonstrate the significance of standard terms in commercial contracts. The second is to argue that greater use should be made of standard terms in legal education. The third is to suggest that the rules and principles applied by the courts when interpreting contracts assume considerable significance in terms of the harmonisation of contract law in Europe. Finally, I attempted, albeit briefly, to demonstrate the significance of mandatory rules, in particular those rules which regulate the fairness of standard contract terms and to suggest that steps ought to be taken, as far as possible, to harmonise mandatory rules of contract law within Europe. The aim of this lecture has not been to solve these issues but to raise them from discussion. The task of the CPO Professor is not necessarily to solve these issues but to raise them and to encourage a dialogue between academics and practitioners. I hope that this lecture will in some small way contribute towards the on-going dialogue and that it will encourage debate on these issues between academia and practice.

SERIE ONDERNEMING EN RECHT

In de Serie Onderneming en Recht zijn de volgende delen verschenen:

0.   W.C.L. van der Grinten, S.C.J.J. Kortmann, A.J.M. Nuytinck, H. Wammes
     (red.),
     Onderneming en Nieuw Burgerlijk Recht, Zwolle 1991.

1.   S.C.J.J. Kortmann, P.J. Dortmond, A.W. Kist, N.E.D. Faber, A. van Hees,
     F.J.P. van den Ingh, A.J.M. Nuytinck *(red.)*,
     Financiering en Aansprakelijkheid, Zwolle 1994.

2.   S.C.J.J. Kortmann, N.E.D. Faber *(red.)*,
     Geschiedenis van de Faillissementswet,
     Deel 2-I   Heruitgave Van der Feltz, I, Zwolle 1994.
     Deel 2-II   Heruitgave Van der Feltz, II, Zwolle 1994.
     Deel 2-III   Wetswijzigingen, Zwolle 1995.

3.   A.G. van Solinge,
     Leeuwe- en andere delen, Enkele gedachten over winstverdeling bij perso-
     nen- en kapitaalvennootschappen, Zwolle 1995.

4.   J. Beuving,
     Factoring, Zwolle 1996.

5.   D.J. Hayton, S.C.J.J. Kortmann, A.J.M. Nuytinck, A.V.M. Struycken, N.E.D.
     Faber *(red.)*,
     Vertrouwd met de Trust, Trust and Trust-like Arrangements, Deventer 1996.

6.   S.C.J.J. Kortmann, N.E.D. Faber, J.J. van Hees, S.H. de Ranitz *(red.)*,
     De curator, een octopus, Deventer 1996.

7.   S.C.J.J. Kortmann, N.E.D. Faber, A.A. van Rossum, H.L.E. Verhagen, *(red.)*,
     Onderneming en 5 jaar nieuw Burgerlijk Recht, Deventer 1997.

8.   J.J. van Hees,
     Leasing, Deventer 1997.

9.   G.A.J. Boekraad,
     Afwikkeling van de faillissementsboedel, Deventer 1997.

10. S.C.J.J. Kortmann, F.J. Oranje, A.A. van Rossum, J.W.H. van Wijk, *(red.)*, Overheid en onderneming, Deventer 1998.

11. S.C.J.J. Kortmann, N.E.D. Faber, E. Loesberg *(red.)*, Corporate Governance *in perspectief*, Deventer 1998.

12. W.A.K. Rank, De (on)hanteerbaarheid van het Nederlandse recht voor de moderne financiële praktijk, Deventer 1998.

13. S.C.J.J. Kortmann, W.A.K. Rank, M.H.E. Rongen, G. van Solinge, H.L.E. Verhagen *(red.)*, Onderneming en Effecten, Deventer 1998.

14. R.E. van Esch, Electronic Data Interchange (EDI) en het vermogensrecht, Deventer 1999.

15. C.M. Hilverda, Faillissementsfraude, Deventer 1999.

16. Gerard van Solinge, M.P. Nieuwe Weme, Gedragsregels inzake een openbaar bod op aandelen, Deventer 1999.

17. S.C.J.J. Kortmann, N.E.D. Faber, J.A.M. Strens-Meulemeester *(red.)*, Vertegenwoordiging en Tussenpersonen, Deventer 1999.

18. J. Stuyck, M. Waelbroeck, B.L.P. van Reeken, S.B. Noë; F.O.W. Vogelaar *(red.)*, Competition law in the EU and the Netherlands. A practical guide, Deventer 2000.

19. S.O.H. Bakkerus, Bancaire aansprakelijkheid, Deventer 2000.

20. C.J.M. Klaassen, Schadeveroorzakend handelen in functie, Deventer 2000.

21. J.M.A. Berkvens, N.E.D. Faber, S.C.J.J. Kortmann, A. Oskamp *(red.)*, Onderneming en ICT, Deventer 2000.

22. I.P. Asscher-Vonk, N.E.D. Faber, S.C.J.J. Kortmann, E. Loesberg *(red.)*, Onderneming en Werknemer, Deventer 2001.

23. J.J. Dammingh,
    Bemiddeling door de makelaar bij de koop en verkoop van onroerende
    zaken, Deventer 2002.

24. S.C.J.J. Kortmann, C.J.H. Jansen, G. van Solinge, N.E.D. Faber *(red.)*,
    Onderneming en 10 jaar nieuw Burgerlijk Recht, Deventer 2002.

25. C.J.M. Klaassen, R.J.N. Schlössels, G. van Solinge, L. Timmerman (*red.*),
    Aansprakelijkheid in beroep, bedrijf of ambt, Deventer 2003.

26. Th.C.J.A. van Engelen,
    Onverkoopbare vermogensrechten. Artikel 3:83(3) BW nader beschouwd,
    Deventer 2003.

27. R.H. Maatman,
    Het pensioenfonds als vermogensbeheerder, Deventer 2004.

28. Ewan McKendrick,
    The Creation of a European Law of Contract, Deventer 2004.